Bypassing Obesity

Sarah-Jane Oakenfull

Sarah-Jane Oakenfull

Bypassing Obesity by Sarah-Jane Oakenfull
First published 2024

Copyright © 2024 by Sarah-Jane Oakenfull

Cover drawing Rosa Beth McDonald
Cover design by Craig Laurenson
Layout by Meg Elphee

All rights reserved.
This book may not be reproduced in whole or in part, or transmitted in any form, without written permission from the publisher, except by a reviewer who may quote brief passages in a review. Nor may any part of this book be reproduced, stored in a retrieval system or transmitted in any form or by any electronic means, mechanical, photocopying, recording or other, without written permission from the publisher.

For C, E, and I

Acknowledgements

Whilst writing this manuscript I have been overwhelmed with enormous support and encouragement from my family and friends.

My husband, Chris, is my anchor, holding me close and grounding me. My daughters, Edith and Iris, have eyes that glow with pride. My parents, Laurence, Carolyn and Sange, have made the creative side of me grow and thrive. Family both near and far have blessed my life so deeply, with full commitment, and I flourish in their palms.

Motivating me daily has been my friends, our laughter and honesty always present. Helen, Sue, Kimberley, KT, Lisa, Tanya and many more.

Thank you, Miriam Margolyes, for being an inspiration to me, your honesty is inspiring.

Preface

Hi there, I'm Sarah-Janes and have carried the burden of morbid obesity all my adult life. As forty approached, I made a drastic but nevertheless much needed decision to change my life and try to live without restrictions and limits, without the burden. At the same time I felt in an important journey to document and to understand the world of health and obsession around food. No one aspires to become morbidly obese adult, it's not a conscious decision.

Thank you for letting me share my story with you all. X

Contents

Have you ever had Chub Rub?	4
Being hugely visible whilst completely invisible	8
Starters, the first season	16
Byproducts	22
Miriam Margolyes and other fantastic, fat, famous faces	26
Travel by car	34
Procreation	46
Society	56
The main course. Grubs up!	62
But you've got such a pretty face!	72
Fat Bottom Girls	78
Controlling the seasons	80
Autumn	88
Bypassing my obesity	98
Obesity bypassed	104
Support in a "C" cup	110
Gaining so much through loss	126
The livin is easy, summertime	134
Moroccan sunset	140
Defying gravity	146
Relationships	154
Hard work and charity	164
The skin I live in	168

ONE

Have you ever had Chub Rub?

If the answer is yes then welcome, my fellow fire-thighs. May the summer be kind and your thighs be smooth. May the cycling shorts do their job, and may the foul smelling, yellow cream that the GP has given you, bring you some relief. Timodine, used mainly for nappy rash and also sometimes for our Chub Rub scalds; an eggy, stinky, cream that brings only a whiff of solace. You are warriors, fighting not only yourselves but society too.

If indeed, you answered no, then please let me explain: Chub Rub is when the meaty flesh just at the top of a pair of juicy thighs (some with what appears like large chicken breasts slapped at either side of said thigh) rub together. Imagine the worst sun burn you've ever had; the kind that blisters, curls and screams like bacon frying on gas. Imagine then, that said-sunburn is between the thighs, just a breath away from your sexual organ. Now grab yourself a cheese grater and with the small "posh" side that you only use when you're trying to impress and appear more sophisticated than you really are, grate the sunburn vigorously. Then, with every step you take, push the dammed grater just a little harder, like you are grating cheese for the sandwiches at a family Christening buffet. Now welcome to Chub Rub. Grated sunburn between the thighs. A constant, stark reminder of the load you are carrying.

Sarah-Jane Oakenfull

My first and one of my most prolific memories of Chub Rub is whilst on holiday in Menorca. We had an apartment on a complex. I'd have said I was about 12 years old. The complex was at the top of a hill framed by tavernas with tanks of fresh lobster, ready to be chosen to meet their maker and fulfill the idealistic holiday culinary extravagance.

Looking back the hill really wasn't that steep, but still, steep enough to raise the heart rate. We had been down to the beach and we, our family of six, were heading back up to the apartment to shower and dress, ready for an evening meal. The air heavy and warm, settling into the last few hours of the day's sunshine, with the lingering smell of seafood paella, sun lotion and fragrant Spanish blooms.

Now, after explaining the sunburn/grater analogy of this oversized thigh byproduct, add some sand into the mix.

Yeah, it ain't pretty nor pleasant, in fact I'd go as far to say it's absolutely and utterly consuming, having to walk, move, make progress, with this affliction. Again, add to the picture a stroppy, pre-teen, with an attitude as big as her left thigh, on her period, bulked up in the nethers with early 1990's sanitary wear and you have a recipe for a pretty shitty evening. What didn't help at the time was a sarcastic dad, two younger brothers, a slim, smart stepsister and a step-mother whom at the time was trying incredibly hard to be understanding, only to have the whole weight of said preteen thrown at her (rhetorically speaking).

I don't remember the meal, only the walk up the hill and some local, rather handsome men and some other holiday makers staring at me as I walked or climbed up that sodding hill with my feet as far apart as they'd dare go, so that my poor, young, extremely tender thighs didn't touch, my dad and brothers actually finding this hideous incident highly amusing. John Wayne disembarking his trusted steed ain't got nothing on me walking up that bloody hill on a balmy May afternoon in Menorca.

Bypassing Obesity

I don't ever remember at any time in my childhood wanting to grow up and be an obese person. I don't believe that any of us (the obese) ever do. It's not something I aspired to become. It was never an intentional decision. Even as I hit my preteens and became chubby, big-boned, and grew puppy fat, all I ever wanted was to be Madonna. Until she did *Erotica*, then I lost interest. Maybe it's all her fault.

This might be a good time to introduce myself. I'm Sarah-Jane, 42 years old, from Essex (I'm not orange and I've never been to The Sugar Hut). An average looking woman, dark eyes and brown hair, although it's been many shades of red, Wella box dyes over the years. I cannot spell for toffee, but I love words. I'm married with two daughters.

This time two years ago I wore a size thirty dress and weighed twenty-three stone. Don't worry, this definitely isn't some procrastinating, self-help, weight loss story. This is just a story, my story, about a woman who wants to share some facts about life as an obese person. A person who has a lot to say on a lot of subjects. I've been both fortunate and not so fortunate to have had many experiences in my life that might just resonate with people, obese or otherwise. We all know someone who is overweight or obese, maybe I can help you see through their eyes.

Having been obese most of my adult life, and morbidly obese for certainly the last fifteen years, has been both a blessing and a curse. Many will wonder how on earth being morbidly obese could possibly be a blessing but it's true to say it has.

You see, I'm a woman that wants, needs, to be noticed and this huge appearance aided me greatly. Along with a loud voice and quite a jovial joke telling, it did the job for me, my obesity.

For many years I embraced the shapes and variety of my bulges. I tried so bloody hard to always look nice and not be a sweaty, smelly fat person. I never adhered to the fat woman's dress of code, the classic black trousers and a top.

Sarah-Jane Oakenfull

Not me, ever.

I was more of a yellow tights and spotty blue dress, cut ever so slightly too low, revealing an ample bust, type of fat woman. I always wore clothes I liked, maybe not always appropriate, but always fun. I'm not one to fade into the background, call me any fat-shaming name you want, water off a duck's back. Call me a Plain Jane and I might just implode.

TWO

Being hugely visible whilst completely invisible

The absurd thing about being so huge is that it makes you completely invisible.
Yes, you stand out. Being one of the largest people in society means that people can't help but notice your bulk. This suited me, as I've said before, I like to stand out and be noticed. I'm a bit of a show-off. On the flip side of that, you are completely invisible. Unimportant, insignificant and almost rated as a second-class citizen at times.

The one who is overlooked when out with slimmer friends, the joker, the token fat girl. It's okay for me to chat with your boyfriend or husband, girlfriend or wife because I'm not a threat. I'm invisible. It's okay to joke and have all the banter with me, safe in the knowledge that I'd never assume you are flirting with me, as I'm invisible. I'm at a busy bar waiting to be served, I'm invisible. I'm in a trendy, restaurant or cocktail bar, I'm invisible. You're smiling and chatting to my friends, you glance past me, a nanosecond, I'm not even a living entity to you, I'm invisible.

This invisibility manifests in so many ways but I'll start with attraction. Now being a member of the biggest in society bracket puts you into a bit of a niche market both sexually and attractively speaking.

Sarah-Jane Oakenfull

There are of course those that prefer a larger, squidgier body to hold, aptly name the Chubby Chasers. I've seen documentaries on this very subject, mainly men seeking women who are very large. They can't seem to get enough of the ample proportions. The feeders that love to watch obese people stuffing their faces, getting sexual gratification from the feast, along with watching the body grow in width and mounds. So there really is a market, sexually speaking for the morbidly obese.

That aside, I myself found that, after getting to a certain size, my attractiveness to others seemed to diminish. I am an over-friendly soul who loves people and will chat to anyone and everyone. But rarely was I approached by a stranger to start a line of communication. I always took the initiative at a bus stop or in a queue somewhere. Usually, it would start with a joke, or a smart remark, just so they know I'm witty, in the hope that whoever it is I'm trying to engage with will like me, and not judge my size alone but take in some of my personality too. After all I am ambiguous, both transparent and completely visible.

The steadfast position I've found myself in, being a morbidly obese woman is that of a none threatening presence. I am the one who has all the banter, the one whom you can have a real good joke with, however dirty the joke maybe. I'll never assume there's an attraction or you have an agenda. I'm to accept my position as a nonentity, attraction-wise. The bubbly girl who always has a smile and a quick quip. Always feeling the need to make people like me and see through the obesity into my actual self.

Now the internal invisibility starts, on every outing or occasion. Whatever the weather, we in the morbidly obese category have to think ahead. Will I fit into that seat? Will the seatbelt in a friend's car fit me? Will the small, wooden, garden chair hold me, or will I crash to the ground with a thud like before (true story)? When holidaying abroad having to ask for a seatbelt extension, *again*, making a joke of it, then worrying that the stranger next to me has enough room as my bottom spreads under the arm rests, causing actual bruises on my hips.

Bypassing Obesity

Yes, we have to have that forward thinking in our everyday life. We have to be ready with an excuse or quip, in order to excuse our size and get in first with a joke, armour adorned and ready for the affray.

Cinemas bring another seating dilemma; the armrests are very uncomfortable to those of us with the hips and bottom of vast proportions. I can tell you that when I went to see a newly released Batman movie, *The Dark Knight Rises*, at two hours and forty odd minutes running time, my hips felt like they had been in a vice (technically they had). I had visible red marks and a deep internal humiliation ensued.

When going into public conveniences the arch nemesis of the obese woman is the sanitary bin. Sitting alongside the toilet, it's a real bloody inconvenience. You see, if you have such ample hips and bottom, when seated they spread. The fat oozes to the sides and takes on a liquid form. Not having any authority on the direction or depth of this fleshy, fluid-like fat makes it very difficult to navigate down onto the toilet seat as you literally have no idea how far it might spread. The sanitary bin has housed my hip and bum cheek many a time, in many a place. Other times you have to physically remove the said bin out of the way in order to fit into the cubical. They are, after all, small at the best of times but add the bin to the mix and it's almost impossible just to do a simple wee. I don't think I ever complained about these things openly, not even to my fat friends. I joked about them and took the piss out of myself, again a form of protection.

When going out for meals, doing a quick visual sweep of the room and with lightning speed, planning your entrance in and escape route out, judging the gap between tables and making a prompt decision about whether the sidewards, arms up to lift the belly mass an inch higher would suffice in order to get through the gap or whether it's the dreaded "Excuse me," apology out loud in the hope the other diners will pull in their chairs.

Lots of us use humour to disguise this and make some self-deprecating jokes, firstly to make sure that the people we're asking to move in know that we know what they're thinking, and get in there first. Secondly, it's an armour. It's our way of protecting our own feelings and let the world know that we are aware of our size. After all we carry it around daily.

Eating out brings another strange set of byproducts. It goes as follows: the over-thinking section; you're out for a meal with friends, and in particular smaller friends, you sit down and the server comes over, you have already decided what you want to eat, you second think it. Your pal, who is of a 'normal' size and stature, has expressed a concern about their own weight. They don't mean to offend at all, to them you are just 'you,' and the size of your body or your food portion size is to no consequence.

They are chatting about it in a throw-away fashion, and it doesn't cross the mind of this average joe that to have to lose a few pounds is completely achievable. To miss out on a larger meal or miss out on a pudding is not a lifelong commitment but a short-term goal. It's within the realms of possibilities.

They order the Caesar salad and no fries, the server looks to you.

In that split second, before a blinked lid crescendos shut and returns to moisten the eyes, you've thought about how it's going to look now if you order the steak (medium-rare with the peppercorn sauce), chips and griddled asparagus spears.

Bypassing Obesity

Will they assume this is why I'm here, taking up so much space? Usually, the said friend would have a dirty burger with all the trimmings but today they are 'being good' and so now, in that millisecond, you have two choices. You can have the meal you want, after all it's only the second meal out this year and you can't really afford it. So have the treat. Or you have a salad too, so's not to appear greedier than the friend, as I'm sure the server has no doubt already assumed. Leave hungry and unsatisfied on this special occasion, my one evening out with a pal that's taken a month to organise, as one of us is blatantly busy when the other is free.

This is indeed a conundrum that we have all faced. So many of us will head for the salad in a bid to be accepted, to fit in and not appear greedy to a stranger.

Of course I get the steak, and I make a joke about it too, "Can't be eating rabbit food, I've got a figure to keep." Now I love salad but if I'm out I want a treat! The jokes continue and if the sever hadn't registered our food choice differences then this is the moment the penny will truly drop. Me: "I'm having half a cow and the fat cow here's having a salad!" They both laugh and I'm satisfied that I've made the point to the server that I know it's bizarre and it should, on face value, be switched, meal-wise. I've let them know that I am fully aware of my size and have ridiculed myself before they walk into the kitchen and inevitably do so. I've made them laugh and so I now feel comforted that they might like me and not be too judgey.

The server smiles and jots down the order but not before asking for our drinks requests. Roll out another byproduct. I don't have fizzy drinks very often but it's lunch time, I have to drive to collect my offspring from school. So I have a carbonated treat, "Coke please."

Here it comes.

I'm nervous for them, the poor sever is going to blush and go and joke with their colleagues about this in a few moment's time. It's building and the hub-bub of the restaurant is creating a backing track for this next round of humiliation... "Is that a Diet Coke?"

Sarah-Jane Oakenfull

BOOM.

They're blushing and they cannot look at me. They stare only at the small pad in hand. The shield of humour engages once again, reload, aim, fire.

"Think it's a bit late for that, don't you?"

Rebound, ricochet, retreat.

I laugh loudly to let the sever know it's okay. Only then will they look at me. Sometimes they'll respond, "I hate Diet Coke myself." Or a little chuckle followed by "Ah you're okay, have what you want". On very rare occasions I've unintentionally really embarrassed some severs. It's never my intention. I love people and merely want to make them smile and maybe like me. I don't want to be that really fat woman on table 12, I'd compromise at the *lovely* fat lady on table 12.

The next issue is this. If I finish my meal first, I appear greedy, as though I have stuffed my face within a heartbeat and it probably didn't touch the sides, particularly if I'm with a slim friend, and they are still chatting and eating, chewing and savouring each tasty mouthful. It might be that they have been telling a story about their neighbour's cat or their mum's hemorrhoids and have taken so bloody long to tell the unnecessary details that I haven't gotten a word in and have just casually eaten my main course whilst they drone on with the spiel. Do I think any onlookers would assume this? Absolutely not. People in general would conclude that I'm greedy and my pal is simply not. This overthinking was at the forefront of my mind for every meal out I had, birthdays and celebrations, with family and friends. With me being the biggest person within my circles of nearest and dearest, I felt it often.

Bypassing Obesity

If I did indeed take my time in devouring my meal, maybe enjoying every morsel and savouring it in all its deliciousness, and I end up finishing after my chums, regardless of their size and stature, it is then assumed that I had a larger portion than said chums. It might have been my turn to spin a yarn, tell a story or let off some steam by having a good old moan about my family or even just chat about Coronation Street's latest story line. Either way I have been talking and my dinner dates have been listening. They've been chomping on their selected feasts, and I've been slowly grazing though small breaths in my communications. They've neatly put their cutlery in the centre of an almost clean plate, and I've still got half of my £15 worth of main course left. If I stop now, I'll leave hungry and would have potentially lost at least £7.50. Also, it's absolutely bloody delicious and I want it, I'm really enjoying it. However, if I don't finish my account of the latest gossip from the important and exciting world of parenting teenage girls I might implode. The server comes over and sees my friend has finished and looks at my plate. Are they assuming that because I'm so big that I'm leaving some on purpose? Do they assume that my meal was much bigger? I haven't put my cutlery together neatly in the centre of my half-eaten meal, the international sign for a meal spent. They go to take the plates. Do they assume I have no manners? The knife is rested upon the side of my plate and the fork has half a new potato, and some flaky salmon with samphire glazed with lemon juice still loaded and ready to be consumed. They go to take my carefully chosen dish, half bloody started. This is the dilemma. Do I say out loud "Oh sorry, I'm not actually finished yet," and embarrass myself and the server? Do I let them take the plate of precious food and therefore falsely admitting I've no manners and clearly have over ordered? In the time it takes for my heart to pump a body's worth of blood through the chambers of the organ, I've pondered on this and overthinking rapidly takes a hold.

Not being able to physically fit into gaps at the supermarket. Having to say, "Excuse me," when trying to fit between trolleys in the bread aisle at Tesco. The overwhelming feeling that you're "in the way" was part of life.

THREE

Starters, the first season

I don't know what is in us, both physically and mentally, that causes obesity to occur. It's not something that is particularly speedy. It doesn't happen overnight. It's silent, imperceptible evolution takes hold, almost like snowfall. The chaos, creeping in without a sound, but causing disruption to the habitual way of life, deafening those who carry it. Yes, becoming morbidly obese is very much like the falling snow: it is gentle, gradual, and sweeps in, waiting to settle, waiting for the conditions to be just right for it to rest and continue. It's like a crisp white polar bear with hyperphagia, the preparation to hibernate during the white, whispering winters. Only it does not cease when spring eventually, inevitably, comes around. No, before you know it, the summer has shone with all its glory and the autumn has blown away the leaves, along with control and hope. The pattern continues, but the silence of the acceleration is always as hushed but steady as the freezing, falling snow.

Towards my last years in primary school is when it began. Very slowly, so gradual that not many close to me actually noticed. I do remember that suddenly my friends' clothes no longer fitted me and so, by the time I started senior school, I was a dress size fourteen.

Sarah-Jane Oakenfull

My wonderful mum, Sange, was a single mum with three children at this point and living on benefits. She had had a pretty hard upbringing financially herself and it seemed that history would repeat. Mum was living in a bubble of grief after my dad had met his school sweetheart and sadly left Mum.

I don't want Dad to be labeled as the bad guy. He is still happily married to my step-mum and very much in love. It can't have been easy for Dad to not live with his young children and must have been an extremely tough decision. I was six, Brett was three and Adam just two years old. Mum was ripped emotionally and had three small children to now bring up alone.

It's only since becoming a mum myself (fuck my life, being a parent is 90% shit) that I appreciate just how hard that it was for her to bring/drag us up alone and living in her heartbroken state. I'm unsure if having a childhood event like that impacted my relationship with food and started my love affair with taste and texture, but it was in the following years that it started to seep in.

As I said, Mum was hard-up financially and, along with her mental health and state of mind, it meant mealtimes were not particularly typical. I remember having vinegar on toast a lot and Mum would make cheap meals and add a tin of beans to make it go further. I hate baked beans. I don't recall sitting down at the table together (although I'm sure we did at times) instead we sat in front of cartoons on the rented, white TV without a remote control. We had an old sofa with a hideous floral pattern and matching curtains. The carpet was pink if memory serves me and there was an old gas fire with stone surround. An imitation gold carriage clock sat on the fireplace shelf in central pride of place. A gold, gilded mirror framing the fake coal, gas-guzzling fire. It was a three-bedroom semi on a large housing estate, the kids roaming free to explore, with one parent or another looking out at times.

Poor old Mum, in her prime at just thirty-something with three kids under eight-years-old, heartbroken and alone. Who wouldn't want an easy life? Here's a quick parenting hack: do whatever it takes to survive it.

Bypassing Obesity

My primary school friends had biscuit tins and crisps in their homes and I used to love it when their mums would offer me the treats. One friend had a mum that worked until five and so we would always go to hers and I knew she'd have snacks. It was starting to become a priority to me to have those treats. It had triggered something within me. School dinners were okay: small portions but always a desert. At home we only had a pudding at Christmas or if one of Mum's new boyfriends happened to want us to like him. We'd be encouraged at school to finish our meal. I rarely left anything, only baked beans.

Dad was very good to her and us, he never let us go without. We saw Dad every Wednesday and every other weekend we would go and stay at his and my step-mum's house, where my step-sister lived also.

The meals were always delicious. Cazza is an amazing cook. I recall having tinned tuna for the first time, and they had three or four types of cheese, mind blown. They were stable financially. I thought they were rich, *four bloody cheeses!* Also at Dad's house was a biscuit tin. It didn't just contain the usual assortment of *Bourbons* and *Custard Creams*, but *Breakaway* bars wrapped in silver foil, like little jewels within a treasure chest. We used to take them and hide the wrappers in between the sofa cushions.

They lived in a cottage that they had restored, and it was very beautiful, very of-the-time, cottage-chic. Sash windows and floral curtains with matching sofa cushions, pine, antique furniture and an open fireplace made it feel very cosy. Having said that, it was never my home.

Sarah-Jane Oakenfull

Next door live an elderly couple. John, a stereotypical old boy, adorned with a flat cap and thick-rimmed glasses, had his garden and won lots of awards for his gladioli. Ida, a very thin, almost poorly looking lady had a gift for baking. The house had the smell of freshly baked Victoria sponge ingrained into the bricks and mortar of the small semi-detached cottage. The cottage was a hoarder's dream and was piled high with old newspapers and magazines. There was stuff everywhere and was just chaos. It was an absolute delight. I salivated every time I went in through the old shabby back door, its peeling paintwork and squeaky hinges. The smell hit you like a brick, I can almost taste that cake now. She only ever gave me a small slither and I always wanted more, sat in the small dining room-come-library-come-jumble sale. Wishing she wasn't so bloody tight.
RIP Ida.

It's a funny old time starting senior school. You are thrown into a situation that brings you to meet others from in and around your catchment area. Slowly, most of the friends from primary years disperse and you gravitate towards your new clan. Fat people seem to have a herd mentality. Speaking only for myself, I've always gravitated towards my fellow chubs. Starting this new big school opened the door to me in regards of this herd of friends. I vividly recall that after a PE lesson, myself and another girl who was of the bigger than average variety, showing each other the numbers in our skirt, *matching sizes,* and the rush of belonging that followed has stayed with me. I wasn't alone in my fatness. It was okay. I had an ally.

It was at this time teachers and students started to call me a name. Not a jibe or putdown. No abuse or micky taking. They kept calling me Tanya. *Who the fuck did they think I was?* As I've said, I gravitated towards the other fat girls and had seen one around, similar size to me, and shorter hair than a lot of girls our age, a bid to be individual away from the excess weight. It transpired that they had been calling Tanya, Sarah. It's common for fat people to be mistaken for others, as society often can't differentiate between common differences, and see only the size, the most obvious thing. It's down to intelligence or laziness in my humble opinion.

Bypassing Obesity

Anyhow, with Tanya being called Sarah and myself being called Tanya, we eventually began to nod at each other in the hallways, as teenagers do. I don't recall who spoke first and neither does she, but we began to say "Hi," then, "Alright?" And soon it became a proper chat. We didn't become thick and fast best mates. It was slow burning. The first few years a senior school you're really experimenting, trying to figure out who and what you are. Those lifelong friendships seem to come after the initial settling in period.

Enter a weirdo called Helen. Helen was so strange. I remember she talked about masturbation openly. It felt like she was trying hard to fit in but also holding a lot back. She was a big girl, with a mass of dark hair, in a group of girls I, at the time, considered a bit square. Nowadays you'd call them normal, but I was a bit of a gobby cow even then. I wanted to be noticed and I didn't give a shit what for. Maybe it was to hide from my size, maybe to embrace it, either way I had a strange view of the normal girls. Helen stood out from them in size and personality. She was honest to a fault. Nowadays I see a kaleidoscope of autistic traits in Helen that round up to a very interesting and complex human being, who is more than just a friend, but has become a necessary organ to me.

FOUR

Byproducts

And so we continue. Along with the dreaded Chub Rub we have a vast bundle of byproducts that coincide with living as an obese person. I'll start with the physical ones as the internal ones will take far, far longer to explain.

I give you the under-belly sores. Some call this the "apron" or "skirt" but in reality it is a belly, tummy, stomach, whatever you wish to call it, that hangs. A mass of skin on your lower abdomen. Depending on your degree of obesity, it can hang really quite low and there have been many a joke/jibe about the mass covering the sexual organ. I didn't seen my vagina for bloody years, although I know it worked. I could perform the relevant tasks that require a vagina. But it was a stranger to me in the flesh, so to speak.

Sarah-Jane Oakenfull

Now underneath the tummy can get pretty warm. In fact it's a fungi's wet dream. The hair follicles can become so damp and compressed that they harbour bacteria and can make some impressive boils and sores. It's not very pleasant but it's a fact of the fat life. Again out comes the eggy Timodine for, as well as the sores and boils, there is the added bonus of an itchy rash. I can remember vividly when I was in my early twenties having an absolute whopper of a boil and sitting on the loo trying to burst the bugger just to get some relief from the discomfort. It burst with the force of an almost opened sachet of sauce (apologies) and hit the bloody door. Satisfying.

We who've carried a tummy mass, have all been witness to this underbelly sore. We have tried talc, unperfumed, PH-balanced, expensive shit. Now, talc and sweat make a very good paste, if ever you need any. It's very durable and easy to whip up. There are the various creams, as forementioned, the Timodine, other nappy rash creams and deodorising sprays, chalks and talcs. All have the same outcome. A waste financially and gaining of nothing. A couple of us tried deodorant, *Sure* and *Mum*, roll on and sprays. *Nada*. A few times I actually put a face flannel under the mass in a bid to beat the beast. It's not uncomfortable as you can't really feel it, but alas it didn't work, it ended up a soggy flannel under my gut as well as a pus-filled boil. No, the only thing I've ever found remotely effective is cleanliness.

As the under belly is so moist it can pack a punch on the old whiffington scale and so I've always bathed or showered twice daily, making sure to dry the problem areas (yes there's more, I'll get on to that) as effectively as possible. Namely, I used a hair dryer or fan. I lift the bugger up as much as I can with one hand and blast the under carriage of the mass with the warm, dry air. Puts the wind up ya sails and manages to give the old pubis a good old blow job too.

Bypassing Obesity

The titty turmoil. Does what is says on the tin. Turmoil, under the pendulous droops of flesh that are hanging on by a thread of stretch-marked skin. The under-udder rash, similar to the belly but spaced out and more rash than boil-laden. Wearing a bra is a fucking insane thing to do, but when you have an enormous bosom its tortuous. Even if, like a lot of us, you opt for the non-wired boulder-holder, they are still bloody uncomfortable to say the least. The boned version of this weapon is, without question, a device designed by a human being with very little or no titty. They dig in, and out. My poor niece in recent years, a very sweet child who adores her aunt, wouldn't cuddle me as the bones in the middle of my bra protruded and very nearly took her eye out. She was not born to be a pirate and so I went back to my 1940's, pointed, non-wired monstrosity.

The under-titty rash is most uncomfortable and not very glamourous. Itchy, sweaty and an absolute inconvenience. I personally would take this however, in place of chub rub or under-belly boil. It's easier to reach and easier to air, i.e. lay down and they spread eagle under the pits, therefore giving light comfort.

Then there is the swelling. Particularly in the hot summer months, I seemed to have feet and ankles in a permanently swollen state. During the summer my feet became enormous and I found it hard to find shoes to fit, so opted for Birkenstocks with the adjustable buckle. When it rained, I'd still have to wear them as they were all I could fit into. The doctor gave me some water tablets once or twice to help, as my poor trotters felts so tight and stretched it was becoming even more difficult to walk. Nothing I tried, no tablets, raising of the feet, pillows under the bottom of the mattress, ice water foot baths, nothing helped to bring them down. It was just purely the stress of carrying such a weight. My feet also suffered around the heels, often very dry and cracked so deeply it felt as if my poor feet were being split open and that is exactly what happened. It was so, so sore and demeaning having to go to the GP time and again, knowing that they would of course, and rightly so, offer dietary and exercise advice. At the time it made the burden of shame and guilt even more dominant. And so the circle continued.

Sarah-Jane Oakenfull

It's all about the knees, hips and back! Not a dance from TikTok but the aches and pains that are often primarily targeted to those areas. The key places that the weight seems to tug at and my god it can make the youngest of us in the obese category feel it too. I often felt like I was in the oversized body of a seventy-odd year old. Groaning and wincing when getting out of the chair, even to roll over in bed was a mission and some nights I would weep at the pains in my poor body.

Another byproduct of obesity is the nighttime, and in fact daytime, toilet trips. With the weight of the body and excess fats pushing around the organs, it pushes on the bladder and so the sack of wee can't fit as much in as intended. The loo break becomes a regular visitor. During the night I'd often have to get up three or four times a night, heaving my body up and down on the quick vacations from slumber.
The list continues but I'll leave it here for now. If you are experiencing any of these things a good GP will help. Ultimately they are the byproducts of obesity. A burden for our burden.

FIVE

Miriam Margolyes and other fantastic, fat, famous faces

It's important to have role models, heroes, or maybe just a figure in the public eye with whom we can identify. For me it is the wonderful Miriam Margolyes.

Miriam embodies exactly what I want and need out of a human being. Honesty, integrity, passion, and humility. I just adore her sometimes-brutal tongue, her truth is a breath of fresh air. The self-proclaimed fat, gay, Jew, she is exactly what it says on her tin, and I admire that greatly. I've always been a great admirer of her craft and have enjoyed her performances hugely. In more recent years Miriam has become an amazing documentary maker and has confronted many important issues, one of these being obesity.

If you haven't managed to see it, I highly recommend it. In the two-part documentary, "Miriam's Big FAT Adventure" she confronts all aspects and stages of obesity and fatness, from those who are desperately unhappy, those who embrace and empower, from childhood obesity to being older. She meets and candidly talks to people from many different walks, those who try all the fad diets to those that choose weight-loss surgery. Miriam talks openly about her own childhood and looks back at what could have started or triggered the fatness. She has a no-nonsense approach that is very much akin to my own.

I'm not chubby or big built, I'm fat! When I watched the documentary, I was twenty-three stone. I found that listening to people's stories from all sides of the fat divide, those who embrace and those who embarrass, really helpful. Ultimately the message was clear to me: health and happiness above everything. If you are comfortable and healthy in your size, whatever it may be, then you are blessed. There is absolutely no escaping the fact that obesity has health implications and by-products, if you happen to be one of the fortunate souls that are fat and healthy and are content with your body then it's my belief that you should own your space, take up your space and be unshakably proud.

Dawn, Jo, and Judy

When I was growing up, the celebrity I was always compared to was Dawn French. I had dark hair and was always loud, cracking jokes and generally being over extravagant with my mannerisms. I one hundred per cent embraced this, as Dawn seemed to have not only humour but sex appeal too. Dawn had that beautiful thick, dark brown bob and would often play the sexy siren or be the one to kiss the guy (Hugh Grant). So when people often said I remind them of her, I was absolutely flattered. So many of us in the fat community are compared to fat celebs, I don't think it takes much imagination to think that two fat people with dark hair are alike in two of the thousands of idiosyncrasies. I know in interviews Dawn said she was often mistaken for Alison Moyet. Again, not very imaginative.

Bypassing Obesity

French and Saunders were at their height in my early teens and were the most famous female comics. They had the wit and inelegance to make fantastic sketches. Dawn always very visually exaggerated and extravagant both facially and with her body. Jennifer, the red-headed counterpart to the dark, larger-than-life Dawn, together were absolutely fabulous (pun). My good friend Haley had shoulder-length ginger hair and we would always be called French and Saunders, even her own son once saw a picture of them in a magazine and said, "Mummy and Sarah".

And so by the time Dawn French became Geraldine Granger in the small village of Dibley, she was already a household name, still big in size and stature and more beautiful and sexier than ever. A true idol for the larger woman. Men seemed to adore her, she seemed to have a respect that a lot of fat people don't always get, most probably because of her talent for acting and comic timing. When it came to fancy dress parties I would always, inevitably, be the vicar of Dibley, an easy costume and I looked the part.

There are other comediennes that come in a larger packet. Jo Brand with her deadpan, alternative humour always delivers. She is completely at ease in her own skin, no pretence, no polish, just herself. Another is Judy Love. Not only is she gorgeous, she is so bloody funny, she's effortless and naturally alluring.

Hattie Jacques being one of the first. Naturally funny and knew how to use her size in order to maximize her bulk and get the screen to notice her, not only for her fatness but also her wit. She was a trail blazer in many ways and worked within the best of British comedy of its time.

Just a handful of incredible talents from the world of comedy, the ones we know and love. Without those wonderfully larger ladies we may not have experienced what it is to see through the size and just enjoy the laughs. Thanks for the laughter and thanks for being us.

Sarah-Jane Oakenfull

Where singing is concerned there seems to be a place for the obese on stage at operas. Many a voice seems powered by size. Pavarotti being the most famous and widely known. Truly special and voice of such magnitude that it's almost frightening. He did his thing and he did it with an ease that most of us in the fat community rarely manage. He had a confidence and was so self-assured in his craft, that the size of the man became secondary to his talent. I think most of us, even if opera isn't our go-to music of choice, can think of a time that we've seen an obese or fat person adorning the stage. It's almost like the world of opera is accepting of talent and talent alone and the visual aspect of the performance is an afterthought. Almost.

I work in a local charity shop as a volunteer and recently an older gent came in to ask if we had any Mamas & Papas CDs. I had a look but to no avail. He told me that he had only just discovered their music and had been entranced by them, understandably. He then proceeded to tell me that he usually didn't like the "fats." He hated looking at them, but he so enjoyed the music that he no longer cared that the singer was a "fat". I stood and tried very hard not to be affected, to react to his comments. Being in a place of work, albeit in a voluntary capacity, it's not acceptable to start confronting issues with elderly folk. However, it did make me think about perceptions and views of others, particularly the older generation who may not have seen or know very many obese people. After all, the obesity "epidemic" is relatively new in its form, and only in the last thirty years have we seen a rise in the weight of the UK residence. It was always known as an American thing to be fat. The old boy who popped in for a Mamas and Papas CD had no idea he was talking to an obese person about the "fats" as I no longer look obese. Still it troubled me greatly to believe that we can still box people up like categories in a supermarket.

Bypassing Obesity

When our lovable cockney girl Adele came along, she shook British artists to the core. We had never heard anything so bloody, crystal pure. She spoke like a cabbie and sang like a fucking goddess. I don't really believe that Adele was ever fat, curvy maybe, or fuller-figured but certainly not fat. Still, it was something of a turnaround for singers of such a high calibre to now include a woman who was of a normal size, a woman who was real and comparable to others. Adele was a truly beautiful singer and happened to be average and not a stick thin model-like waif. Her voice came first and foremost, her personality and accent second and her frame last. It was refreshing to have such a relatable public figure, in both meanings of the word. Of course, nowadays Adele has slimmed down and she seems incredibly happy but again the media made a frenzied "Adele looking beautiful after shedding the pounds", making those of us living with obesity feel like outsiders. Not that I blame Adele for that at all. Happiness is the key to living, whatever size you are, as long as you're as healthy as you can be and are happy then hats off to you.

In my youth it was mainly American sitcoms that seemed to play host to any fat actors that I could identify physically with. The likes of Roseanne Barr and John Goodman, maybe that's where the chubby and cheerful persona of the larger person came from. The bubbly girl, as I was always known. It seemed that almost all actors or indeed public figure that are fat seemed to be funny, maybe a coincidence or maybe just typecast. In fact, as I sit here trying to wrack my brains for any serious, fat actors I can only think of Kathy Bates and my dear Miriam. I'm sure there are plenty more, but I'm hard pushed to think of any.

I know that a historical and important figure was Mary Seacole, a British, Jamaican nurse who during the Crimean War set up a hotel on the battlefront to treat soldiers wounded in battle. She provided hot meals and when the money ran low, she wrote of her many travels to help pay for the hotel. Pictures of her show a large woman, a true hero and important figure in British Black history. Mary was, for her time, a hero and defiantly an inspiration to the fat community.

Sarah-Jane Oakenfull

Of course we could include Henry VIII, a very obese man. Known for his size and of course his many wives. Not really a historical persona you'd want to be inspired by or look up to at all. All the same, a very well know obese man of importance in British history.

Historically the large and fat people in society where often seen as the wealthier ones and indeed in times gone by, when food was fuel and not an indulgence as it has become now, it was defiantly seen as privilege to have so much to consume that you had put on weight.

If you think about it, us, the human race, are just mammals. As mammals we should have some sort of reserve, genetically we need a covering, a back-up, in case of emergency, illness or famine. If we saw another mammal looking thin and bony, we would instinctively feel emotive towards the animal. We see the super slim, models and celebrity culture and we compare, our children compare. When did we as mammals accept that these thin versions of ourselves were seen as the beauty? It baffles me to think over the years we have evolved ourselves to believe that our species need to be so slight with no reserve or back up. Who decided this? When we look back at the finest art works of the eighteenth century, the women, although not fat in any way, were covered and curved. Healthily so.

Look at the fine work of Lucian Freud, the coveted painting of the obese woman on the settee, curls of curves and drippings of substantial flesh. The lady of interest is looking not serene or even particular relaxed, but like she has been hit by exhaustion, or similar to a mum who has had a long hard week, as well as looking comfortable and not ashamed of her body. That painting has inspired me many times. I see a true woman, a human being, I see a part of myself in her and I see the beauty in her slumped drapes, almost like her dripped flesh is taking a bow.

Bypassing Obesity

The Kween, Lizzo. Oh my god, Lizzo is as sexy as they come. Her talent and her persona shines so freaking bright that you'd need sunglasses just to meet her. She is the sexiest artist of our generation, and she just happens to be fat. Lizzo is an inspiration, and she is so unashamed about her body that she makes us other fat people happy to be in her category. I have a great admiration and respect for Lizzo as an artist but also as a human being who just happens to be fat.

Back to Miriam. My respect for Miriam comes from a place of recognition. I love people, as I've said. I'm interested in how they think, why they reacted to life and situations. I enjoy hearing about lives, loves and losses. I truly believe if we all listened to each other more, learnt about how why some of us think the way we do, help educate the people that need it. Particularly where obesity is concerned, education is key. If people understood what life is like as an obese person, if we could clarify that we didn't ever aspire to become an obese person. The choice was ours mostly, but subconsciously, not an open choice that so many think it is. If the hate was taken out of fatness, if the laziness and stigma of sweaty, smelliness was eradicated, would society then take the time to learn and help us, instead of the judgmental stereotyping that plagues us every day? We all need to listen and us, as obese human beings, need to talk openly and not hide in the shadows worrying about what others are thinking. Easier said than done, I completely understand. I think that's why I decided to write, to explain, to educate and hopefully inspire, the way that Miriam inspires me.

Miriam also loves people, the way she speaks to other human beings on her travels, she would treat "prince and pauper" alike, no difference to her if you are any particular colour or creed, race or religion, sexual orientation or gender. She is so inspiring, I just wish we could all be more Miriam and call a cunt, a cunt.

SIX

Travel by car

I passed my driving test after six attempts. One of those I had actually turned up on the wrong day, a day late to be precise. On one of my tests, the examiner actually tutted. I had done several major faux pas. I mounted the curb on one of the instances and forgot to turn off my indicator for about 10 miles after a junction. Bit embarrassing now I think about it actually. I've since passed and am a competent driver.

Cars have always been a bit of an issue for me. One friend had a little old Peugeot; its seat belt was too small for me, it literately would not go round me, it was a good few inches from the clip. Sat in that grubby, blue, little tin of a car, worn and weathered interior with an old, smoked in from owners gone by smell, I felt a shame deep within me. Of course, I laughed it off as I always did.

On my driving lessons with my second instructor, a very calm and patient woman, I would always make joke about my size. It was almost to spare myself and the lovely lady any embarrassment.

Sarah-Jane Oakenfull

As those that are currently in the grasp of obesity know, the gap between the tummy and the steering wheel is sometimes a millimetre or two. For others, myself included, it was a case of no gap at all and I had to adjust my sitting position to allow my roll of lower stomach fat to fit under the wheel so I could steer safely. When one is vertically challenged and has short, stout legs it was nigh on impossible to reach the pedals and fit the tummy under the wheel. Take that and the full extension of the seat belt into play and you don't have much, if any, room to manoeuvre yourself. So once you are in your safe, optimal driving position it's very tricky to then have to move. When reversing I found that unless I could learn to rotate my head 360 degrees, like a wise old owl searching for prey in the dead of night, I would almost certainly be forced to readjust my position, and this made me even more nervous. You simply have to look behind you when reversing, it's non-negotiable.

In the end, my lovely instructor managed to talk to the test centre and it was agreed that when and only when I was reversing, I could unclip my seat belt so I was able to shift onto one hip and take the relevant check behind me. Now I'm writing this it seems so improper, but this is what I had to do in order to be safe enough to pass my test.

The next issue I have with transport in my car is the seat belt yet again. Because my hips and bottom were wider than the seat itself, they tended to overspill. When you're a driver or a passenger, the clip for the seatbelt is a weapon. It jabs you like a boxer in the ring, only this fight is for the entirety of your journey. I always had a dip in my hip with a lumpy mass just above it where the fat had been pushed up, like when you've been wearing socks with a pattern all day and the indent to that pattern remains. Only because I drive a lot or tend to be in the car for sometimes long periods of time, the indent remained from the clip and has only recently diminished.

Bypassing Obesity

The feeling of this strange, lumpy mass and indent was often like having an invisible bruise, nothing was seen on the skin itself, just a deep bruised feeling along with a crushing realisation that yet another physical by-product had developed through my morbid obesity. Again I would laugh this off, my armour went up and I'd crack jokes about it to my family. I can't even fit in the car appropriately, ain't I silly?

Having some family that we try to visit a few times a year, four or five hours away, and my own dad now living two hours' drive away meant that these long journeys became less sporadic and mostly a monthly trip. My hip would be on fire by the time we arrived and the relief of unclipping that belt was like cool water rolling down your back on a scorching summer's day. The indent would feel deeper and the mass of fat above it even bigger. The sacrifice I had to make for my obesity.

On journeys that involve not just your immediate family but an extra, I did however have an advantage. I was by far the biggest, therefore if I sat in the back, that didn't leave much room for the plus one, so I had the roomy front seat with all its leg room and full access to the music and climate control at my disposal. The kids or adults we were ferrying had to squish into the back like sardines, whilst I, the whale if you will, had room to come up for air. All the while drowning in self-loathing and feeling like my hip might displace.

The road rage is real in this one. I am, as you might have concluded, a swearer; Swearer-Jane. Being in the driving seat brings out some of my most colourful language.

I am by now able to judge a distance and almost always know if I can fit though a gap. Years of table weaving though busy restaurants and bars, predetermining if I can fit in places and spaces has served me well, and being in the car is no exception. It infuriates me when drivers cannot seem to see how wide the gap is. "You can fit a bus through there," is an average, daily affirmation in my world, along with the odd F and sometimes (regularly) the C word too.

Sarah-Jane Oakenfull

My dear daughters are immune to the shock of swearing, it's not something I'm proud of but I just love words and there are occasions that only a fucking good swear will do. The downside of being vocal on the roads is it's not uncommon and very often it's reciprocated by the unimaginative, "FAT BITCH" response. Honestly do these people think they're the first to have called me fat? It doesn't even register any more mate, get some education, and learn some more exciting nouns.

Flying is by far the ultimate humiliation when travelling as an obese person. Firstly the murmurs from fellow holiday makers, "The plane won't stay in the air with her on," "Hope I don't get stuck next to her," "She needs her own carrier plane," are just a few of the comments I've listened to over the years, travelling as a morbidly obese passenger. I'll take this opportunity to refresh and remind the reader that although I am indeed very large, I am still very much a human being. I bleed.

Now I've said that my defence was always humour and a few times on flights I would say loudly, almost proudly, almost, to the air flight attendant, "May I please have a seat belt extender, please?" Always with a smile and always very politely. I want people to like me, to see though any preconceived ideas they have about me. I'm not lazy or smelly or rude. I'm Sarah. I'm fat. The staff always very kind in a busy, rushed way. Trying to deal with screaming babies and older people that hate screaming babies, toddlers kicking and over-excited children on repeat, "But how does it get into the air, Mummy?" "Will we see God?" etc. Other times I would quietly pop on my call button or wait until they are doing the rounds of check, to almost whisper the words: "Seatbelt extender." I guess everyone has days when they feel overconfident and can ignore the criticism that others emit. Other days they feel almost embarrassed and introverted about the space they take up.

Bypassing Obesity

When the seatbelt extender comes you can feel the glances and hear the echo of other passengers' thoughts. It's almost as if you are projecting your own shame on these people and it has rebounded. I always feel like I know what they are thinking, and it makes me uncomfortable. In my mind they are thinking, "Well look at the state of her, having to have an extension for her seatbelt!" As they clip up their own strap. It's always a topic of conversation with fellow obese people, and I'm sure that other passengers don't think that much at all, they are most probably just thinking of their own holiday, but we as obese, tend to overthink, especially after years of comments and opinion.

The next issue I have with flying is again the size of the seats. The old hip indent/mass comes into play. If you are sitting next to a stranger the likelihood is that your hips, thighs, and bottom is spewing out from under the arm rest. The arm rest is nesting on top of your hips, or in some cases, like on one particular flight, just won't come down at all. The poor hostess even tried to push the damn thing down herself onto my ample hips, but I ended up wincing in pain and had to fly with my arm rests at half-mast to Crete.

Another time when going to Majorca we had the box type seat with no arm rests just little compartments for the passengers' middle sections. This was truly uncomfortable as I just didn't fit and had to fly with my body at an angle, resting on one hip so I could get the bulk of my mass into a seat. The air attendants again, very kind, until I discovered that my lap tray didn't come down. I don't mean all the way down, no; it only came down about three inches. There I was, sat skewed on the side, with my tummy pushed up like Dolly Parton's breasts in a Wonder Bra.

That was mortifying.

Sarah-Jane Oakenfull

It truly was a shameful day. The hostess that had been so kind when bringing me the extension and trying to help me fit into a comfortable position was becoming a bit exasperated with me now. In the end she went out the front where they keep all the duty free and heat the plastic trays of in-flight meals and came back with a cardboard box. She held it out to me and suggested that I use the box upside down as a table. I don't know what to write next really.

This day was up there in my jar of obesity memories that cut very deep. The man whom I sat next to wasn't a chatterer. That didn't help, bless him. I don't know what he must have thought of me. To the other side sat my husband, with his lap tray down and my drink as well as his upon it. I fought back the tears and can still taste the salty indignity of that flight. At the time I thought it might be my wake-up call to kick start some sort of weight loss program but, as it turns out, that wasn't to be the case at all. I am a human being and that day I didn't feel very human at all; I felt like an inconvenience, and it was all of my own making.

On our honeymoon we went further afield and embarked on a long-haul flight of nine hours. Unfortunately, we checked in late (a running theme), and we were given seats apart. Now usually I'd have at least one person next to me that I know and love. So whoever is the other side, and although it's embarrassing to have your bottom spewing onto them, at least you have your partner on the other.

On entering the aircraft, I spotted my seat, and my heart sank. I was sitting beside three young lads, maybe about twenty years old. 'The poor blokes,' I thought to myself. I slipped on my protective cloak of humour. I approached almost laughing, "Sorry guys, you're stuck with the fat bird." I then went on to make a bit of a scene about the seatbelt extender, saying about it being my honeymoon and what a lucky man my hubby was to have such a babe as a wife. The lads turned out to be lovely and didn't seem to judge me or look down on me at all. They ended up in the same hotel and called me '*Mrs O'* all fortnight.

Bypassing Obesity

From one aisle to another, the aisle of the aircraft. It's narrow. The small journey to your seat from the entrance of the aircraft is done by using a dance-like-walk. I'll call it the crab. It's a sideways shuffle of a dance, and the dance has lyrics to match. The step sideways along with the apologies make quite a show. The aisles are so very narrow that I couldn't fit down them, so I adopted the sideways crab. The trouble is my stomach protruded, almost as large as I was wide. But the tummy is soft, so I manage to squeeze myself along the aisle like a giant crab, clawing peoples' shoulders with my belly as I went. That happened every single flight I went on in my adult life.

Just to finish on the air travel front is a nod towards the facilities. The loos are very snug. I've often wondered about the mile-high club and pondered if anyone who is fat has actually ever managed to join the gang? It's hard enough to get in, let alone take down your trousers or lift your skirt. Then to have to drop your undies and bend down to the loo, knees hitting the door and belly almost to the floor, hips and bum kissing the side walls. How on earth two people have enough room and leverage to perform a sexual act is just beyond me.
I've opened the door and nearly knocked out the cabin crew too many times to count, having to open the door fully to get my bulk out. Being fat made me very clumsy. I was always bumping into things, people, tables, toilets.

The train has a similar story toilet-wise, aisle-width wise and also has a by-product for the obese of its own. The seats with tables. Really if you can fit in one it's just a glamorous boob holder for us girls and maybe a bit of top tummy too at a push. Trains tend to be a little more comfortable than planes and cars, slightly wider seats, if you manage to get one.

Floating with style

Now boats, buoyant as they may be, are the obese nemesis. I recall one afternoon at the end of summer when my first daughter was just a baby, going out with the family on a lovely little rowing boat downstream in a small Essex village.

Sarah-Jane Oakenfull

We had queued for some time and my anxiety levels were increasing with every minute. I honestly thought that every person that saw me in that queue was waiting to watch me try and get into that bloody boat and ultimately see if it would hold me. I'll never know if that was the case.

When it came to our turn to set sail, or row in our case, my husband took our daughter bundled in a blanket and my brother and sister-in-law boarded the boat.

My turn.

Holy moly.

I, of course, made a joke to the young lad who was manning the rowing boats and asked loudly if he was sure that the small boat would hold me.

I was about eighteen stone at the time and a dress size twenty-four-ish. The lad held the boat steady, or as steady as a rowing boat on a moving stream can be. Now it was my turn to step on board.

Deep breath, I slowly lifted my right foot and tried to heave myself down onto the vessel. One wobbly foot landed on the boat. I think, if we are honest, the boat dipped into the stream quite considerably. However the dear little wooden boat, adorned with two oars and three neat little wooden seating benches stayed afloat and it embraced me as I quickly and heavily, fully embarked the vessel.

We ended up having a fairly nice hour just doodling up the river. The memory of getting into that twee little boat remains one of shame for me and I didn't enjoy the experience as much as I should have, just worrying about what other people were thinking of me.

Bypassing Obesity

I have a deep, deep love for the Isle of Wight. My friends and I have had some ladies-only mini-breaks there. It blew my mind at just how beautiful it is. You do of course have to get on a ferry to get there (or hovercraft, but alas I'm not that wealthy) so I drove to Portsmouth and boarded the ferry.

The first time we went, we were late, a running theme throughout my life, and I ended up parking skewwhiff and not being able to fit out of the driver's side door. I had to climb over and get out the passenger side, not an easy feat when you are twenty plus stones.

When we got out of the car and made it onto the main body of the ferry, we realised that ferries, or this ferry in particular, have many, many steps. Good lord, we very nearly passed out by the time we got to the drinks cabin.

Another time I recall being on top of the water was at a church day out. My mum being a regular churchgoer invited us along too. We went to a local loch with the happy clappy crew, who had a supply of canoes to use.

Reluctantly I decided that I did fancy having a go really, and somehow managed to get in the bloody thing. A blue, light weight canoe with a sit in the top style set up. At the time, not at my heaviest, I must have been about eighteen stone or so, one of the men "in charge" held the vessel, and whilst I joked about getting in and the floaters ability to hold me, I lowered myself in. It did hold me, and I happily had a go, skimming across the water, laughing and joking whilst feeling almost weightless and buoyant.

Then came the time for me to get out.

Oh dear Sarah.

I managed to get to some old metal steps on the side of the steep bank of the loch. Everyone was busy and no one seemed to notice that I needed some help to disembark. I called out and husband came over but was unable to help from the edge of the riverbank, looking around for someone, anyone, to come to my aid-in-water so to speak, to hold the damned canoe whilst I attempted to heave myself up and out.

Alas no one came.

After what felt like three days, and total shame and humiliation, I actually had to capsize myself to get out of the long, thin, floating vessel, and then swim over to the ladder. Quite a spectacle for the church as I'm pretty sure I made a few expletive remarks at the time. I didn't ever go on any church days out after that.

In the Isle of Wight there is a beautiful cove, hidden, and apart from on foot, it can't be accessed. I walked there one year with Helen She was very patient with me as she's quite fit for a fat girl. Steep Hill Cove is very aptly named, I thought I might die that day after walking there and back.

Yes, boating is a bit of a bitch to the obese. But mainly in our own minds rather than reality. After all we, in general, seem to float, us fatties.

Travelling without moving. Not a 1990's album by a man in an oversized hat but what is also referred to as *walking*. Having two daughters and a dog means that I have to go for walks. I am an outdoorsy person. We love the beach and the woods. I take my children to parks and make sure they have more outdoor adventures than screentime. This involves me walking.

Walking is not easy when you have twenty-three stones to carry on a small frame. Every step is an effort. Every yard is a struggle. Not for everyone, some obese people are fit, healthy and very able, but for me it was intrinsically difficult. I found myself making excuses not to walk so far. Making the girls run with the dog, sitting by the park whilst they played.

Bypassing Obesity

I dreaded having to go to the toilet round people's houses that had a loo upstairs, knowing that I'd have to get up the stairs. I can't describe how hard it is to lug a body upstairs that is so very heavy. I suppose I could liken it to feeling deeply tired, like you've done hard graft, then put on jeans, a t-shirt, a thick, woolly jumper, big heavy boots, a winter coat with bricks in the pockets, then you've been dunked into a pool of water, so everything feels substantial and laden. To lift a leg is an effort, then to push the other leg up along with the burdened torso is almost agony to boot. A small walk felt like a marathon but it was something that simply had to be done and so I pushed myself to walk every day. It was slow and progress was even slower. I got a Fitbit and made sure I did as close to ten thousand steps a day as I could.

Walking was not my friend but, other than swimming and sex, it was the only exercise I had. You could never have called me a lazy, fat person. I did more than I could do. I pushed my heavy body to move and I'm so glad I did. I know people that have such painful joints due to not moving more. It becomes so hard thereafter to restart the body into moving that it's near on impossible. Unfortunately it becomes a downhill snowball after that as the pounds stay on, or pile on, and any form of exercise becomes impossible.

Like I have said before, obesity doesn't occur overnight but is a gradual process. It's never a conscious decision to become so fat that moving is a struggle. Sometimes it's a compulsion to eat. Mental health can play a part too. Ultimately, it's individually discreet but finding food irresistible and like a drug is a self-soothing mechanism. Finding the effort to move when you are morbidly obese is something only the strong-willed, bloody-minded do. Unless, like I've stated before, you happen to be fat and fit. I'm a bit of a martyr in some respects and made myself do it, just so I wouldn't be classed as fat and lazy, so I would be respected in a way.

SEVEN

Procreation

It is said to be estimated that one in five pregnancies result in miscarriage. When I look at those numbers it sends a shiver down my spine. One in five. That's an incredible amount. I have suffered two miscarriages, both before I had my daughters. When you are in that situation the numbers don't mean shit.

It's not something that's widely discussed in our general society and so the estimate doesn't seem to fit. Knowing that you're one of five others doesn't even scratch the surface of elevating the grief. It's all-consuming and envelops you like a foggy mucus. Smothered in the sticky, rank slime that's impossible to simply wash away. If I had been one of a hundred percent of women going through it, I wouldn't have been able to soak away the devastation.

The first miscarriage I suffered was at seven weeks.

At the time I was about eighteen stone. My husband and I had decided to try for a baby, and I was lucky enough to fall within a year. The elation was instantaneous, from the second I saw that line on the plastic, flat figured oblong I was a mother, a protector and I felt like I had won the lotto and conquered the earth all in one moment. I felt like I was the first person to ever have gotten pregnant and was fiercely protective, extremely proud and felt a glow from deep within myself.

Sarah-Jane Oakenfull

I found out early, as is often the case when trying to conceive; you test the day your period is due and so can find out as early as three or four weeks. I proudly made a doctor's appointment disclosing to the receptionist that I was expecting and a few days later I'm almost smugly telling my GP about my positive result.

So, I was booked in for my twelve-week scan for eight weeks' time and told to take folic acid, although in truth I had already began to take those, revelling in what a wonderful mummy I was even at such an early stage.

I carried on working but was careful. At that point I was working as a care assistant at a home for the elderly. I worked with some great co-workers who seemed really pleased for me and so I had a few weeks of bliss. I was being supported by my colleges and my family were all absolutely thrilled. I'm the oldest of my siblings and so this would be the first baby in the family for some time. The fact I had no morning sickness or any of the usual symptoms of pregnancy just fuelled my whole "mother earth" ethos, I was quite literally made for this.

Then very randomly and with no forewarning, I went for a wee and checked the loo roll, as many women do when pregnant or not. I noticed that the tissue had a strange colouring to it. Then it started to happen.

The end.

The pregnancy was over, the baby that was no bigger than a pip from an orange was gone or going. Over the next few hours I began to bleed heavily. The crimson of the blood matching the deep, dark scar appearing in all chambers of my heart, my soul.

Bypassing Obesity

Someone once said to me that I probably wouldn't have known that I was even pregnant or miscarrying and would have just thought that my period had come if I hadn't found out so early. I disagree. When miscarrying it's not simply a heavy period but much more than that. It's not just a collection of cells or the lining of the womb coming away, it's a heavy, painful experience. I did know I had been pregnant; I did already love my baby. I'd already mentally named it and chose a pram and breastfed the beautiful creature subconsciously.

I googled. I shouldn't have, but I did.

On the NHS web page it states that a pregnancy may be more likely to end in miscarriage if you:
- are obese
- smoke
- use drugs
- drink lots of caffeine
- drink alcohol
-

Now at the time I was a smoker. However, the moment that second line appeared, I quit. I haven't been a drug user and had the occasional glass of wine and drank about five cups of tea a day, no fizzy drinks or caffeine-heavy beverages. The top reason for a more likely miscarriage is obesity. That was me. I was morbidly obese. Had I done this?

I called the GP, and they referred me to EPU, early pregnancy unit, at our local hospital. For me it was an utter emergency but to them this was a daily occurrence.

My husband drove me over and we booked in and sat and waited. We waited and waited. We waited to see a nurse.

After a few hours and several toilet trips in which the obvious miscarriage happened, although I remember her being very kind, she was very used to this and tried to reassure me that this happens to many, many women every day. That it was nothing that I'd done wrong but just natural.

I did another pregnancy test: positive. Hope?

She explained that the pregnancy hormone can stay in your system and could take weeks to show a negative result, but I'd be referred for a scan to check that it was a full miscarriage. Unfortunately, the doctor for the ward was extremely busy and so I was sent home and given an appointment for a few days' time.

The journey home was quiet. Tears came and dried. I was numb and powerfully intense all in the same moment, the deepest grief ever felt. I desperately clung on to the hope that my test was still positive and thought that perhaps I had been carrying twins and had miscarried one baby. I hoped that it had been just a bleed and that the tiny pip was still clinging on. But deep within me I knew. When you pass a miscarriage, it's painful and apparent. It is not like a regular period or clot. I knew and I knew why. It was my weight. I had caused this.

I'd like to add here that this is how I felt in that moment and have since accepted that it happens to "normally sized women" too. It can happen to any woman at any time and most often has absolutely no rhyme or reason.

I'm trying to find the words to describe the grief of losing a baby, however small or early the pregnancy was. It was all-consuming, like living in a bubble filled with fog, add to that a profound, immeasurable guilt so intense that it's like swimming in the deepest blackest ocean inside that bubble of fog, unable to surface. If I could pop the foggy bubble, maybe I could float up and face the guilt-ridden grief but it seemed impenetrable at the time.

I did eventually see a glimmer of light from the surface, maybe an angel fish showed me the way back up, but the bubble started to disperse over time and the fog became thinner.

When it came to our follow up visit, I had to have an internal scan. It's almost degrading. Laying in a shallow pool of grief, bleeding the remnants of your baby and having to have a doctor insert a scanning machine into you. I have since had many internal scans and have become hardened to them now, but that first time was not pleasant to say the least.

Bypassing Obesity

The doctor did her examination and exclaimed that I'd had a full miscarriage but there might still be some "product" to pass. "Product." That word haunts me. How can losing your baby be referred to and ended with that word? She was a small, insensitive woman, who had most probably worked too many hours and seen too many women lose their babies. It was just another statistic to her. I felt like she knew that it was because of my obesity and was being harsh with me for causing it.

By this time I had turned to my first true love, food, and then on to my another of my go to crutches: cigarettes. For the obese or fat, or indeed just some of us in this huge world, our one true solace lays in food. Something in the hand to mouth action brings me comfort. The excessively salty and the extremely sweet seem to sooth me momentary.

Feeling how I did at the time, it might have been, and many people said so, that it was the perfect time for me kickstart a healthy lifestyle and lose weight. Needless to say, that did not happen.

If you are an alcoholic or a drug addict, in times of despair you are drawn to your weapon of choice with a vengeance. To block out the hurt and pain, the addiction thrives on misery and uses sadness as its vessel. Addiction is a complicated illness and it's just that, an illness, a disease.

My weapon of choice, or maybe not a choice as such, but my weapon was food. I hit it hard, the equivalent of bottles of vodka or lines of cocaine, packets of crisps. Easy to obtain and far, far, cheaper than class A drugs. Couple that with legality and the physical need to eat to survive, and the mixture was completely achievable for the addiction to take hold and consume me. Then the guilt set in a little deeper and the addiction to feeling full and satisfied devoured me. I so desperately wanted to get pregnant and try again, the more I ate, the more guilty I felt about losing the baby and being so obese. The more I ate the more the feeling got buried temporarily.

This continued for several months, eating, grieving, guilt and desperation in a cycle. Then I fell pregnant again.

Elation. I slowed the eating down with a self-control I didn't even know I had. I didn't eat healthily per say, but I didn't sit and eat multi packs and whole pizzas. I thought about my tiny passenger and made slightly better choices, food-wise.

I started to feel sick, great sign apparently. My boobs hurt and all was looking and feeling very positive. We didn't manage to get an early scan, even after the miscarriage. In my area, only after three devastating losses are you considered at risk and so are able to access the early scan and be monitored closely. However I called the scan department and managed to get a slightly earlier one at eleven weeks instead of the usual twelve.

The countdown began. Every toilet break was dripping with dread, expecting to see signs of a miscarriage. Every twinge, ache or slight discomfort was over examined and dissected. I read the pregnant book section in every free second and googled each step of the gestation journey daily. Too scared to make love or overexert in anything, I was on light duties at work and wrapped myself in a transparent cushion of hope and desperation.

The day came and we sat in the waiting room with two other women, one heavily pregnant, feeling an almost buoyant optimism edged with sinking apprehension. We were called in and I had to lower my trousers and lift up my top, lay on the bed and be covered with jelly. As the sonographer pushed down the mouse like tool to search for our baby, I vividly remember her apologising that she had to apply pressure. She asked me to lift up my tummy. The tyre of fat seemed to be obstructing the view of our precious cargo. I did as she said and in the darkened room, I felt her sliding the mouse around my lower abdomen whilst I held up the mass. She searched around in a silence that could break glass.

Eventually she said the words.

Bypassing Obesity

I don't remember when I let go of my tummy and let it spread back out to cover the place that my baby lay. When I think about it now, it feels reminiscent of a padded curtain enveloping the foetus. It's almost a comfort. Almost.

I remember looking at my husband and feeling like I'd let him down again. The sonographer led us back to the waiting room, the heavily pregnant lady looking very uncomfortable as we sat down, me sobbing like a child, for a child.

After some phone calls and paperwork the sonographer came back, and we were taken back to the early pregnancy unit again. This time was different. Much more intense.

My tiny passenger's heart had stopped beating at nine weeks. I had been carrying the elfin sized gift for two weeks without even realising that the flickering ember of life had gone out.

We were given options at this point. Let nature take a natural course and take time to miscarry the baby, while going about my normal everyday life.

I thought about the waiting, the sight of blood and the agony that continue to grip us whilst we waited. The second option was to return in the morning for what they called an evacuation of the pregnancy, a medical procedure in which I'd be under a general aesthetic and wake up no longer with my passenger.

Now this is an individual choice and decision to make but I felt like the lesser of two evils was the latter choice and so we got booked in for the next day and given some leaflets and left for home.

Another silent journey, with tears as loud as a hailstorm on a tin roof.

Sarah-Jane Oakenfull

The only things I remember about that evening is laying in the bath, holding my tummy, crying so hard that the water went tepid. I could have drowned in those tears. I lay in that bath for a long while, having some time alone with my baby, talking silently to it and apologising profusely for not being enough for it to thrive. I tried to hold up my vast tummy and touch where the sonographer had applied that pressure so I could feel as closely as I could to the place my baby lay, the only place it had ever been or would be. I was in the bath as I said and found the task of lifting the mass of tummy tricky. I couldn't lay my hand very successfully upon my baby's place of sleep. Although fat is squishy and adjustable to some extent, I couldn't do what I wanted to do and just lay my hand upon the sleeping morsel, through the vast layer of fat that felt like it was keeping us locked apart.

Guilt.

Again.

My husband and I held each other tightly that night, no words just comfortable silence in our most uncomfortable situation.

Then morning came as it inevitably always does.

I had to get up and have a bath, get dressed, put one foot in front of the other and walk down the steps to our car.

I didn't want to. If the baby just stayed where it was then at least it was still with me in a sense.

Bypassing Obesity

Deep down I must have known I was making the right choice having the procedure. For me personally I don't think I would have dealt with another visible miscarriage emotionally. And so we got into the car and drove back to the early pregnancy unit, again. We were then sent to a ward, the gyno ward, where they booked me in and gave me a bed. I had to put on a gown and wait. Everyone was kind and understanding. I was eventually taken down and remember counting down as I fell into the deepest of medicated sleeps. I woke up crying. Asked if my dad was there. I'd had a dream that I don't remember now, but it was about my dad. Then I asked if my baby was gone.

A kind nurse, replied, Yes.

I was so upset, teetering on hysterical, so they went and got my husband and when he appeared next to me, he just held me, united in grief.

Fast forward to being at home that evening, bleeding again but like a light period, rather than the visual miscarriage I'd had before. We just stayed home alone and chatted about nothing and everything, had dinner and a bar of sweet chocolate, watched TV and went to bed. Exhaustion-induced sleep came, as we held each other.

The weeks and months after just rumbled on. I ate all my feelings, cementing the guilt like a stone carving of a hideous beast, me. I had decided that for my own emotional wellbeing and the sake of our family that I'd go back on to contraception for a time and let myself and husband grieve and hopefully heal somewhat. We felt like having a baby was something we needed to be stable and secure in our own minds for, particularly as the more miscarriages you have, the more likely the next pregnancy is to be fated too.

EIGHT

Society

How the vast majority of society views fat people, and indeed the obese and morbidly obese, interests and confuses me in equal measure. The way we are treated and the overall preconceptions and opinions towards us, the people that are largest, throughout our lives, can be extremely hard to stomach (pun!).

With the likes of Katie Hopkins spouting her venom in our direction and some random model that no one has heard of, making headlines in the UK's grubby tabloids for saying how much she hates us, it makes me wonder how alone they are in their small thinking patterns.

I've spoken about the invisibility of obesity whilst being the largest in society. Have these women opened a gap in the door for those that are subconsciously already carrying this hatred towards us? And if so, why? To face this I'm going to have to rip off the plaster and find out why these people feel that way.

One plausible reason is cost. On the UK Government website it states that "obesity is projected to cost the NHS £9.7 billion by 2050 with wider costs to society estimated to reach £49.9 billion per year"[1]. It also states that "the costs of the annual spend on the treatment for obesity and diabetes is greater than the amount spent on the police and fire service plus the judicial system combined."

Whilst typing this I'm completely astonished and, yes, feel that old gut-wrenching guilt and shame seeping in. It's a very hard fact to face that by me eating so much and allowing obesity to control me, I've contributed to these figures. However, at this point I have to reiterate that not one of us in the grasp of obesity has welcomed its clutches and none of us invited it in or sought it intentionally. One does not aspire to become obese. It's not an option that we have consciously taken. I didn't wish to become obese as a child.

This being said, I have to explore the medical issues that obesity breeds and aids. The main concern is usually diabetes, high blood pressure leading to heart condition and stroke, some cancers. For example, as an obese person I'm three times more likely to develop colon cancer than that of a healthy weighted person. Along with that, there are the smaller complications such as creams and lotions for sores and chub rub, gallstones and stomach issues, sleep apnoea, fatty liver disease, and the list goes on.

---

[1] https://www.gov.uk/government/publications/health-matters-obesity-and-the-food-environment/health-matters-obesity-and-the-food-environment--2

One of the most overwhelming is that of mental health, thus creating a cycle of guilt, shame, desperation, and despair. Mental health and obesity don't always go hand in hand, but it's fair to say again that most of us don't actively choose this path and so it becomes a heavy burden to carry mentally, as well as physically.

According to the Priory Group online it states that "despite there being a number of demographic variables that could affect the direction and / or strength of this link, including socio-economic status, level of education, age, gender and ethnicity, a 2010 systematic review highlighted in a two-way association between depression and obesity. The review found that people who were obese had a 55% increased risk of developing depression over time, whereas people experiencing depression had a 58% increased chance of becoming obese."[2]

So basically, those who are obese are half as likely to develop depression and those who have depression are half as likely to become obese, than those that do not.

All of this was found pre-Covid, and so I may be correct in my assumption that the up-to-date percentage could be even greater.

I find this astounding and it's made me wonder why, after living with obesity for my entire life, am I only just learning this? I will revisit the impact of mental health and the effects of obesity on our state of mind further on.

For now, I will continue to explore why those so called 'Fat Haters' might feel we are such a bane.

"Fat people are so sweaty"

Having been morbidly obese my entire adult life, I have to say this comment has legs.

---

[2] https://www.priorygroup.com/blog/the-relationship-between-mental-health-and-obesity

Being large and heavy, covered in a thick layer of fatty tissue does make for a warmer body temperature. Moving it requires much more effort than that of a small frame thus using more energy, thus creating more heat, that then produces sweat to cool off the body. Small things like walking the kids to school had me taking off my coat in winter because I became overheated and would sweat profusely, walking up the stairs and up hills would turn on a tap of sweat.

Now I consider myself very clean when it comes to personal hygiene, and shower or bath twice a day. Obviously I use a deodorant and have clean clothes daily. I never could wear the same item of clothing more than once without washing it. So, I have never smelt. I have however been very sweaty and uncomfortable.

Some obese people struggle immensely with sweating and with bathing or washing, so it's inevitable that some and only some obese people have the whole smelly, fat thing going on. This doesn't mean that they are dirty or unclean, but it does mean that they are struggling with the everyday things most take for granted.

To tar all fat people with the sweaty, smelly brush is unjust. However, we are looking at why some people in society have such a hatred for fat and so this could very well be a by-product that we can take heed of. It is after all true, no escaping the fact that fat people do sweat more that the smaller in society. To see any person on earth sweaty is unpleasant. Most activities that involve sweat are unpleasant… most. So, it is to be expected that it's an unpleasant sight. Add to that the sheer size and amount of sweat coming from a large body after doing, let's face it, not a marathon but a small walk or everyday task can be frustrating to a fat hater, almost unsightly to them.

Bypassing Obesity

Attraction then comes into play, along with sweating. Now we all have a "type", perhaps a celebrity we feel most attracted to, or a deep longing for. I myself find beards very attractive. Some like blonds, some like guys heavily built or effeminate, some like women that are strong and bold, some like big boobs or a Jennifer Lopez bum. We all have a thing that we find attractive in other human beings, physically.

Some of us have things we absolutely do not find attractive, for me its long toenails. This doesn't mean I have a deep hatred for every human being with long toenails, but it's something that would put me off, so to speak. Some people can't get enough of the fat figure, and I can understand why. It's squishy and safe, warm and comfortable. Some people find this form very sexually attractive and crave it. There have been many a documentary about 'chubby chasers' or 'feeders'. They can't get enough of the vast rolls and huge bumps.

Then there are those that are attracted to a very small frame, some who long for an androgynous frame. Some who just love all shapes and sizes on offer.

People who have a preference for the very petite and are put off by the appearance of a big body can be disgusted by the fat form and, as I've said, we all have a thing that we love but also loathe. For some it is fat. Add to this the appearance of a fat person sweating then yes, I can see why some would be shocked by the outlandish concept of attraction to that form.

But to hate a human being on their appearance is not a concept I can gel with. Would I hate a person solely on how they look? Would I hate a person if they happen to be wearing, say, a top that I really didn't like? After all, they can change the top and thus become more pleasing to my eye. I suppose that the fat haters would reply that becoming our size, obese, was of our own doing, and to some extent they are right, however as I've stated time and time again, it was never a conscious choice to become morbidly obese.

Laziness...

Okay, so yes, to the fat haters, we are a herd or group of human beings that have eaten too much, cost a fortune, sweated all over the shop, unattractive and are ultimately just lazy, right? Let's just see why they might have that opinion.

Yes, moving is harder when you are very large and, yes, it most definitely makes you move slower. Fact.

Did I sit on my bottom a lot shouting at the kids instead of getting up and diffusing situations? Yes.

Did I knowingly become lazy? No.

Was every bloody step, every climb, incredibly hard work? Yes.

Did I still walk daily? Did I still take my children to the park, go to work, do the shopping, gardening? Yes, I did.

It was harder for me at twenty-three stone to do all those things, than it is a half-marathon at nine and a half stone. Carrying such a lot of weight makes everyday life harder. Yes, from an outsider's perspective it looks incredibly lazy, but to someone who has lived with obesity and knows the struggle it's most definitely not laziness, but a grapple to do the simplest tasks. So again, I'll state, it was not a conscious decision to become morbidly obese. It happened so gradually and with such stealth that I feel like it had stolen me, very slowly and steadily.

I would ask anyone who sees just a fat lazy person to adorn some weight, maybe give someone a piggyback ride for a day, or put some tins of beans in coat pockets or try anything to temporarily add some bulk to your frame, for a decent amount of time, and just move, do everyday things: stairs; gardening; etc. See how it feels to carry this burden, then see how lazy we are. Everything is harder. Everything takes more effort, more time and willpower, endurance to do. The laziness you see is struggle and it is out of necessity in our current situation and not out of a pre-empted decision we made to become this way.

NINE

The main course. Grubs up!

Okay, so I can't write about obesity without talking about food. After all it is an integral part of being obese. The ultimate part.

Right then, I'm going to start by having my say on food-related issues and then touch on other angles. For me, food is a drug. It has been my main concern and first love, it's my go-to in times of joy and sadness alike. Food has filled gaps that nothing else could. It satisfies and completes me.

I have spoken briefly about addiction. I've not stated that I'm addict myself, but I am. The way the illness grasps and melds you, and the speed at which it does so, is astounding. Addiction to alcohol or drugs is a recognised illness, rightly so. Food addiction seems almost implausible. Maybe as a society we've not been ready to accept it, but it does exist, and it really stands up as a true illness.

The manifestation of the illness isn't just one of gluttony or overindulgence, but seems to take on different guises. Like in all addictions, one size really does not fit all.

Sarah-Jane Oakenfull

In 2019, I went to a music festival with my husband and two daughters. We camped for three nights. I was about twenty-one stone and very large, about a dress size twenty-eight.

It was incredibly hot and the festival involved a lot of walking. To say I struggled was an understatement. My feet had swollen, bigger than ever. I hardly fit into the camping chairs and I awoke in the morning on a damp, lifeless, air mattress that had diminished considerably during the night. I had no sleeping bag as I didn't fit into our single sized ones and was wrapped up in a duvet from home. The showers were very tight for room, as were the toilets. I managed and we did have a fantastic time, but something changed within me that weekend.

I'm a music lover and the atmosphere at the festival is right up my street. It's my absolute happy place. I sat, squashed into that camping chair, feeling bruised at the hips, hot, swollen and basically just felt fat. I felt every extra pound that my body was carrying. I sat in the chair, not able to easily get up. My girls had to pass me what I needed, my husband had to help me up and out of the chair. I could barely walk for ten minutes without needing a break. My family are supportive and were to some extent used to it, but it had never been this apparent to me. They were almost caring for me on that camping trip. It hit me so hard that I felt an internal misery. That misery ignited an ember that began to grow in the coming months and years.

It was then that I decided that when I got home I'd explore myself and try to figure out just what the actual fuck I could do about myself and how to be kind enough to myself to find change.

Now at this time my brother had been through rehab. He has since been sober and has learnt to live with his illness and take control of it, rather than it controlling him.

Proud.

Bypassing Obesity

It started me thinking about food and slowly I began to wonder whether it is possible to be addicted to food, to feeling full and to flavour and texture alike.

Like many of us do, I googled. I found a group that is under the same premise as the incredible Alcoholics Anonymous Twelve Step Program. The group ran every Tuesday evening in a town hall local to me. So one evening I decided I'd go and explore the notion that food could be an addiction. I attended Overeaters Anonymous, bravely solo, not knowing what to expect. *Would it be a group of fellow fat people sobbing about?* Turns out, no, not at all.

The group is as stated in the name: *anonymous* and so I won't divulge more than to say that food addiction can affect anyone, at any time of life. The illness of food addiction can take on so many different forms that I'd never even considered. I thought it would only be other fat people complaining about being fat and moaning about being so. If I'm honest, that's pretty much how I felt.

In the group there where so many different characters, ages, sizes, from so many walks of life. Some were alike to me and my own size and food related issues, some were recovering from eating disorders and some just beginning to admit they had a problem. There is a large number of people who have a referred addiction to food after giving up drugs or alcohol.

Some can be addicted to one food or food group. For example, crisps seem to be a food that can have addictive appeal, chocolate or sweets is another. We crave these foods normally, all of us at some points have fancied a bag of crisps or a taste of chocolate, so what happens when that fancy begins to become a need? The answer is: I honestly do not know! I suppose what makes a person go from enjoying a glass of wine in the evening to needing a bottle of vodka a day just to function.

Sarah-Jane Oakenfull

The issue with food addiction is, that unlike with drugs and alcohol, you have to eat, to survive and thrive. A human being can live and function without drugs and or alcohol, but no human being can live without food and nourishment. It is an intrinsic part of our survival on earth. This is not to say it's a harder addiction to battle, but it certainly requires another added affliction to deal with, the one of self-control and the old friend moderation.

During my times at the meetings I learned three important things:

I wasn't alone in the way I felt about food and my need for it, quite the opposite actually. There are so many people out there struggling with the same obsession with taste and flavour and the need to feel overly full to be satisfied, most of whom still think that that's a natural way to feel. If you happen to be one of those, help and support is out there, just a quick google away. But it has to come from you, and you have to be ready to face your own addiction.

The next thing was: a food addiction doesn't automatically equal obesity. Like I've already said, the others at the meetings that I attend came in all shapes and sizes. I had believed that an addiction or deep need for certain food just literally made you obese and thought perhaps that was the answer to the obesity problem. I was wrong.

The last thing that struck me was a bit of an oxymoron. I had an excuse. Well I can't help it, I'm addicted to food. If I ate four cream eggs a day, it wasn't my fault, I have this affliction, this illness, in which I have to eat and feel so physically full it sometimes hurts. This was a dangerous thought but made me extremely self-aware at the same time.

Bypassing Obesity

An addiction is not an excuse or a get out of jail free card which you use to escape your behaviours. Addiction is a non-negotiation disease that consumes you slowly. It's not something that can be thought of as an excuse, to eat in excess. This made me question my own addiction altogether and made me question whether or not I was even addicted to the consumption, or just looking for a way to normalise or excuse my eating. Or was this a part of the addiction itself, manifesting as an excuse? It really is a minefield; addiction and eating disorders are so very complex that it's impossible to pick apart the psyche of it all, so I won't even attempt to. What I will do is explain my own eating habits or addiction, my need for certain foods and my overwhelming need to feel full to an uncomfortable capacity.

When I was a child, my mum would sometimes let me stay up late. Being a single parent I suppose sometimes she liked the company. When we sat and watched TV together, we would often have a chocolate bar and packet of crisps. I believe this was the start of, like for so many of us, the association with food and feeling special, or a shared, important occasion. Sat watching *Dallas* or *Come Dancing* with Mum. Watching all the beautiful gowns swaying with every fancy dance step, I felt so grown up and those memories are so sacred. I enjoyed the treat too, although back then it wasn't a need, just a craving. It was the icing on the cake (pun!) to have those snacks, the main attraction was just being up late and spending time with Mum.

When the small parade of shops on our estate opened a new Chinese take away it was like Christmas. The sweet, salty, sour bright pink sauce with chips was usually all Mum could afford but my god, it was heaven. Because we didn't have much money, food was fuel and not really anything particularly tasty (sorry Mum) and so when I had these new flavours it was like a taste sensation.

Sarah-Jane Oakenfull

My mum's good friend Eileen had two boys and I would spend a lot of time at her house. She had an open-door policy that meant you could go in and have what you wanted. Eileen had a goodies cupboard, a crisp cupboard and always had fizzy in the house. Eileen introduced me to spaghetti bolognaise; I remember it like it was yesterday. The most divine thing I had ever consumed, Eileen wasn't stingy with her portions. In fact she was a bit of a feeder. That suited me perfectly. A huge plate of bolognaise and garlic bread; at least once a week she would make that and she always did me a plate full. She also liked to make deserts and I'd go round and we would make all sorts of delicious treats: a rice crispy, toffee, chocolate thing, scotch eggs from scratch. It was a treat to be at Eileen's house and because she didn't have a daughter, it felt like she was a surrogate mum to me back then. I'd go round and moan about mum to her and she'd feed me.

The differences between my mum's house and my dad's foodwise seemed to gather momentum as I got older. I suppose Mum was cooking on a tight budget and was an old-fashioned cook, thick gravy and throw in a tin of beans to make it go round. In stark contrast at my dad's, we had joints of beef, pink in the middle, we sat at the table and had to use napkins. We ate very well at Dad's, and it was always a "posh" dinner, salmon or barbecues with a number of salads to go with the home-made lamb kebabs and butcher's sausages. The differences didn't occur to me as a child. It was the norm to us that at Dad's we had all this posh stuff, and at home we had normal boring dinners, or a round of toast for dinner if we'd had school dinners.

Later, when I was at senior school, we had free school meals and we would be given a dinner ticket, us Poor Kids. It was worth £1.20 per day if memory serves. I would usually get seven packets of space raiders, those being only ten pence at that time and also a cake of choice. I'd started to develop the habit of eating a large amount of crisps and it soon became normal for me to eat all seven packets and not even acknowledge that it was an overindulgence.

Bypassing Obesity

And so, with my new normal being instilled to my psyche, anything up to ten packets of crisps was completely acceptable to me. As I got older this never wavered. I knew in reality that this was very much not the average consumption of crisps, but it became so normalised to me that I shut off that part of my subconscious that told me it wasn't.

Crisps are my heroin. They are my bottle of vodka. Crisps are my weapon and my release all in one hit. The more I had, the more I wanted, just like the drugs above. There is something about the salt, the crunch, the flavour that satisfies me deeply. Crisps are like an old friend that comes and soothes me when I'm down, and smiles with me when I'm up. A turn of phase I keep finding when researching why we have this need for certain foods is "hyper-palatable." I suppose this makes sense. Hyper meaning over-stimulated or obsessive, and palatable being the taste or eat-ability. Crisps are most defiantly a hyper-palatable food, as is chocolate, for me at least.

Like with the weight gain, the food addiction was gradual. It started as far as I can remember as a feeling of fancy and, for a while, I could go to sleep at night having not had what I fancied. I don't remember when or why it became a need. There was no defining occasion or incident. I do remember however small snippets, from early teens into my twenties, when the need took hold and I had to have these foods. However full I felt after a large meal, I could always manage a few bags of crisps, and always needed something sweet thereafter.

In my early twenties I got a takeaway pizza one evening and some coleslaw. We really didn't have much money at this stage, and it was a treat. That pizza was so thick and greasy, it was salty and soft. The coleslaw was homemade with a substitutional amount of mayo. The taste and textures were divine and soon I'd be thinking of that meal all day. I got into a habit of having that meal three or four times a week. We couldn't afford it and I'd have that one meal rather than shop. Eventually, and thankfully, the pizza place went out of business and so alas my fling with that obsession had to come to an end.

Sarah-Jane Oakenfull

As time went by, my meals got bigger and the more I ate, the bigger I got, the more I needed to feel satisfied. Still after large meals, I would need my crisps fix every day. On average I'd have at the very least two or three packets and a chocolate bar to finish.

In time, the fear and panic began to settle in and my addictive thoughts became louder. Sheer panic, like the panic you feel when you have to slam on the breaks when driving on the motorway. True, real, physical nerves, like a fizzing in your blood or boiling in your chest. It bubbles up from the thought of not having those salty, crunchy snacks. It became very normal to me. I'd get a family pack of six or ten packets of crisps, and they would be my evening snack, after my large meal, then followed by a sweet, smooth chocolate bar. On those times I couldn't attain my savoury drugs, I would head to the kitchen cupboards and scan them like I was hunting for gold. The next best thing to crisps was a cream cracker with butter and Marmite, giving both crunch and salt.

My life was almost fully dominated by my need for crisps and followed by the sweet fix too. I had some beautiful meals, all be it very large, but I've always eaten well. Homemade chilli and rice, the beloved bolognaise. I love Greek food, Mediterranean foods, lots of vegetables, meat and fish. Heavy on the carbs as it's cheap. Risottos and chicken with blue cheese sauces, goats cheese tartlets. I've had many a steak, rare with all the trimmings, every meal was followed up with the crisps and the sweet fix, no matter how full I was.

I've always had a thing for Cream Eggs and in 2015 I started having two in the evening. Then I'd have one during the day too, before I collected the children from school.

At this point I'll say that I have a child with additional needs who is a superstar but very hard work, both physically and mentally. I was just under twenty stone and my daughter was a runner, a climber, in fact she still is.

Bypassing Obesity

Anyway, I began to have a Cream Egg sitting in the car before I did the school run, a little treat before the onslaught. It worked out far cheaper to get a six pack so to speak, rather than just one or two, and so after a few days I'd have two and save the rest for the evening. Before I even realised this habit had taken a hold I had rationalised it in my addict's brain: *I deserved this treat*. And although I knew it was extremely unhealthy, and let's face it, abnormal, I was eating at least six cream eggs a day and at least six packets of crisps. The fear of not having them soon overrode the thoughts about health and weight.

The seed of obsession-addiction had grown and was no longer a seed but a flourishing bloom, a heavy weed in fact.

I started to hide wrappers. I tried to throw away foods so I couldn't snack. I will admit I have taken them out of the bin and eaten them. I remember one evening when my husband was in the bath, I ate a sharing packet of cashew nuts covered in thick salt. Then, when I heard the roar of the plug and the bath draining, I hid the packet under the sofa. All the time still having my usual packets of crisps. If one day I'd only had two or three packets, I'd feel like I'd been really very good.

One time I had got my six pack of cream eggs and we had one each, my husband and me. We went to bed and I couldn't sleep, all I could think about was those eggs and I was quite literally salivating. I got up at just after 2:00 AM and ate two. Almost satisfied, I went back to bed. The next day I had to get more to replace the ones I'd had during the night, but I ate those too and so it continued and on and on, until that festival.

At overeaters anonymous, I spoke openly about this. It wasn't until I sat telling absolute strangers that it really hit me like the end of a rolling pin in a bowl of digestives readying for a cheesecake base. I really had a problem.

I was addicted to these foods. I always will be. I had to try to manage this. I had to lose weight. I had to live free, firstly of food controlling me and secondly, free of morbid obesity.

Sarah-Jane Oakenfull

I want to ask a question that I've asked myself and lots of other obese people. Are all, if not most, morbidly obese people addicted to food? There is no right or wrong answer. If there is, I certainly don't know it. I am torn between both answers, as indeed they are. Surely we have to ask why and how it's been left without aid for so long. Equally if it's a no, then why and how have we, as a society, not addressed some sort of reason as to why obesity occurs.

TEN

But you've got such a pretty face!

I think most of us obese people have had this or something similar said to us at some point. Strangers, acquaintances, family or friends, it doesn't matter whom, has uttered the words. They all assume that it's a fair comment, meant with respect. I mean really it's a backhanded compliment, "By the way, your face is okay but, my god, your body is a train wreck!" People who haven't lived with obesity or even fatness have no idea that those words can be so very cutting. If you are of an average size and happen to have something on your body that you dislike and mention it, has anyone ever said to you, "But you've got such a pretty face"? I assume not, although maybe they have, if so, I apologise.

It seems to be the phase that people cling to like it's a generic compliment to the largest in society. Maybe they feel as though they have to pick some sort of positive out of the negative bulk.
So can we in fact be fat or obese and beautiful? My personal opinion is absolutely, yes. As an obese woman I felt confident some of the time and wore sometimes outlandish clothes or clothes to show off my best assets (boobs). I often felt beautiful and although I was most defiantly in a niche market attractively speaking, I demanded attention and got it. Not always good attention, granted.

Sarah-Jane Oakenfull

There is a community for the beauty in obesity, the BBC's, Big Beautiful Women. It's a breath of fresh air to see these women embrace the curves and bulges they have and the confidence they ooze. I've often looked up to them and classed myself as a BBW. I wanted to be in a group of women who accepted and embraced themselves as individuals in a world the expects a standard size ten. I felt like I stood out and shone in my own way. Now I can only speak for myself, but I didn't always feel that deep down. I was struggling so much with the physicality of obesity that the message got lost and I couldn't shake off the feeling of shame and guilt, particularly after I had my daughters. For those women and of course men that truly feel as ease and comfortable in their bodies, however big or small it may be, I commend you and wish I had truly known it.

So, beauty is in the eye of the beholder. It's subjective, like works of art. Some find fat very attractive, like I've said before; others do not. The real question here is, do you find it, fat, attractive on yourself. Do the by-products of obesity hinder attractiveness to you?

Look in the mirror on a good day, a day that you feel attractive and important and ask yourself and only yourself, Am I attractive to me? You are after all, the only person on this planet that knows you!

At times I was desperately unhappy as a morbidly obese woman but other time I felt glamours and very attractive. I wore clothes that aided my body and felt like god's gift some days. However, I always felt it, the obesity, like a blob of chewing gum stuck on your best coat, not able to be simply washed away. An irritant, even on the brightest days.

Other days I felt nothing but shame, guilt, and a deep desperation, particularly when I started struggling physically. The mountain I had in front of me was of colossal proportions and I could not see a way around, over, or, indeed, through it. I was stranded in obesity and my expedition was bigger than my love of clothes or standard in dress and so I often wept, self-pity and guilt tears stinging my cushioned cheeks like bitter, cold, mountain air.

Bypassing Obesity

Clothes play a huge part in this and as I've already said, I have a passion for clothes not only fashion-wise, but clothing yourself to suit your size and style, projecting yourself through your chosen outfits. If money was no object, then I would have happily left the house in some random, but personality-driven, outfit every day as an obese woman. I tried desperately to not blend in with the whole usual fat woman's attire of black trousers and a top. Quite simply the cost of plus size clothes makes it very difficult to have a varied choice of outfits and it's only in more recent years that the choice has become a more up to date fresh look, rather than the older lady style. I saw "looks" and loved them, but that didn't mean they would suit me, or even if such garments were made for the sheer size I needed. Coats were always a problem, so very expensive, and even my love of charity shops waned as most of us obese find something we love and wear it to death, having to make the most of what our money has provided. The jeans I owned lasted little more than a year, as with leggings. This is because of the chub rub syndrome. When we are bare-legged the chafing is skin-on-skin, thus creating the burn. When the chaff is fabric-driven it wears and wears and wears until holes appear like stars in the night sky, until you reach the black hole effect, and the garment has simply evaporated.

These were sad days for me, saying goodbye to my favourite clothes was hard. They had served me well and held my thunder thighs apart. *My Protectors, farewell, may you rest in peace, fair fabric*. Tops and dresses lasted much longer and I loved to layer up. A roll neck, shirt and cardy, with a colourful scarf was my go-to in the winter. Leggings were a staple but never just with a t shirt, ever! I felt I got my money's worth with tops and dresses and would sometimes find the odd piece in the chazzas, as I like to call them. These chazza shop finds in plus sizes are like rocking horse shit and I'd be elated when I made a find. I often would buy something even if I didn't much like it, just because it was my size. Then I'd try to style it out, mismatching it with something random to make myself more individual as a fat woman.

Sarah-Jane Oakenfull

Yes we have certainly come a long way on the plus size fashions and with the likes of Scarlet & Jo, Shein, lindy bop, Simply Be and many high street shops providing a range of decent threads for us to wear it was an expensive pursuit and I like many others spent way beyond my means in an effort to look and feel good. I ended up in a pickle with it, financially. These days life is expensive, and clothes are, after all, a necessary component of living. I was trying to fill a void, the void between myself and the mountain. I tried to fill it with clothes that made me feel temporarily better. The mountain didn't waiver. The mountain didn't budge. The costs got bigger and so did I, then the costs got even bigger. The clothes I wanted so badly to reflect my own self-worth externally were just so damn expensive.

Now I hear you saying it and I totally agree, 'The bigger the clothes, the more fabric required.' Therefore the price has to be reflected as such. There truly is not much one can say about it really. It is what it is.

So I had looked in the mirror and thought that the woman I saw was attractive, but only when dressed in a certain way, a way that I struggled to financially pull off. The mirror was so honest and sometimes unkind. Some days I seemed to really see myself and other days I'd see what I wanted to see; I was an oxymoron. On the days I felt the self-loathing I would try and make an effort, a bit of lipstick and a dress. My go-to outfit was a navy and white spotty dress with yellow tights in winter and bare legged (cycling shorts for the chub rub) in summer. I was trying to make myself embrace the obesity like I'd seen so many women in the BOW community do. I'd post on all my social media platforms quips about curves and beauty. I would share pictures of beautiful fat women and hope the "likes" would indicate a reassurance, resonating with me. I felt like I was on a mission to make obesity exceed and embraced. This was all before my physical struggle, it has to be said, although deep down I wasn't unwrapping the whole chocolate bar, just a tiny corner of it, in the hope I'd start to believe my own memes.

Bypassing Obesity

The truth is, whatever outfit I wore, posts I'd share, whatever I said to embrace obesity, it was still a burden to me. It wasn't an aid nor blessing. Obesity was consoling me and devouring me, slowly, and this front of almost-pride that I was exuding was in fact a façade that, at the time, I fully believed. Alas I was just re-closing that tiny corner of the chocolate bar. I wasn't actually ripping it open and seeing its dark brown, sweet glory at all, I was hiding it, just like the wrappers of the foods I was hiding too.

Keeping your true feelings hidden deep down is like melting butter slowly. It begins to liquefy in your mind and eventually the solid is nothing but oil. I tried so very hard to justify my size and embrace it. I believed in my own statements for *fat girl power* and *big is beautiful.* I still do believe that fat can be beautiful, but it got to a stage in my own life that the fatness, obesity, was hindering me and I could no longer look in the mirror and see a bombshell beauty, only the overwhelming struggle and hardship it was causing me.

Clothes were papering over the cracks. However many outfits I had, and whatever colours and personal statements I was trying to project, I just couldn't hide the fact that I couldn't get up the stairs without feeling like I'd exercised for the day. Clothes didn't ease the pain in my joints, they no longer diminished the niggles of aching in my hips just to roll over in bed and clothes didn't moderate my mind.

I felt done.

I was ready.

ELEVEN

Fat Bottom Girls

Aah, Freddie said it best. *Fat bottom girls you make the rocking world go round*. After all I've said about the horrible and sometimes unbearable by-products of obesity, there are positives and social views that can reinforce the "plus" side of not being slim.
I'd like to real iterate what I've for said about health. As long as your health isn't suffering and you, yourself are happy, healthy, and wholesome, then keep rocking the world with those fat bottoms. Now this song was a 'go to' in our house. On busy, stressful, shouty mornings or manic bedtimes, in times of chaos and anger, the Alexa would often be asked to play, Queen, *Fat Bottom Girls*, and it always brought a smile.

TWELVE

Controlling the seasons

I've heard people refer to life in seasons, childhood being the first season, the events of which shape and almost define your life, compartmentalising those early foundations that ultimately set your path. That being said, I know of many individuals that have had traumas, such deeply troubled childhoods, but have become warriors, survivors and are some of the most fearless, dedicated human beings. The seasons follow and the events and circumstances get put into various other seasonal compartments.

If this is the case, I may be in autumn now. I hope this isn't winter, the bleakest chill.

I suspect that I started with spring, as we all do. Immaturity and innocence aiding the proverbial, energetic spring in our step. Food being my stepping stones towards the next season. Getting a taste for what's to come and normalising the foods that made me feel good.

Sarah-Jane Oakenfull

Summer being the time of life that some of us bear fruit and bloom like the bedding plants, all pretty and colourful. If this right now is autumn, then it really was a long summer, having gorged with almost a predictive glance into hibernation. I was riding it out and laying down the fats, ready for the long winter, hypothetically speaking. Unaware that I was doing so and clearly unintentionally. I was a big, brown bear in that season, readying myself for the long winter.

Towards the end of the summer period of my life, came a realisation that hibernation isn't a definite, natural process. That's when I actually woke up and smelled the sweet, summer roses.

If I were an animation, a huge, glowing lightbulb would have adorned my head like a halo, and possibly there would have been a klaxon too. The end of my life's summer season was sat/squeezed into that foretold camping chair at a music festival. This was the moment that defined, developed, and ultimately turned the first leaf a shade of fiery, autumnal red. Somewhere, possibly in my subconscious, it had been brewing like a mulled wine, a warmth in the coolness. All of a sudden it hit like the effects of the bitter alcohol, and I started to feel just a smidgen freer. As the dregs of summer passed by, I struggled physically but continued to lay down the fat reserves as I had been since the first warm days.

However, the light bulb did not flicker nor fade. It was now, with autumn approaching, that I now had a hunger for a better life, and I wasn't going to let the light switch that powers the bulb above me to be flicked off.
I tried again.

Slimming World.
Weight Watchers.
Basic healthy living.
Calorie counting.

All to no avail.

Bypassing Obesity

The larger your stomach, the more hunger hormones you tend to produce. Not an excuse, merely a fact of science. I wasn't ever satisfied, and diets were like walking one hundred miles through thick, black molasses to me.

I walked more, tried really hard to be more active, a huge struggle when you are carrying the weight of two average grown men around in one body.But the more I tried to move, the more my body needed to recoup the effort and fuel the body to do so. Having said this, the light above me never wavered, in fact it just seemed to glow brighter, like my very own my lighthouse in the storm. This was I suppose, the eye of the storm at the end of summer. The warm air had ignited an almighty storm and here I was right in the middle of it, not a beginning and certainly nowhere near the end.

I had seen my GP about my weight too many times to mention. I had gained support from health professionals and had counselling. I had gym memberships and one-to-one support from a lady within a healthy, living team that was part of a government scheme to help families become healthier in both physical and mental health aspects.

I had tried and exhausted most options.

Did I try hard enough? Probably not, being completely honest but I had given 75% of available options a go. When you live with and carry obesity daily, sometimes you cannot see the woods through the trees and the task is simply too big, too obese.

The GP had twice recommended me for weight loss surgery and twice been rejected on the basis that although health-wise negative consequences were almost inevitable, at the present time I had none. No life-threatening health by-products on the list that a smaller, average, I'm guessing healthier person had deemed essential, ticks on a chart that can start the process of WLS (weight loss surgery) on the NHS.

These include: diabetes, sleep apnoea, high blood pressure.

Sarah-Jane Oakenfull

You have to have, and be able to prove that you have, exhausted every other option within the dieting and exercise realms and have struggled to keep weight off.

I will come back to this. Right now we are in the eye of the biggest storm that my life as a fat worm has ever seen and I'm hungry for change.

Now we are not a rich family, my husband, daughters and I. We are not struggling to excess but we are sometimes robbing Peter to pay Paul. I made some calls anyway.

I made calls to private clinics. Clinics that offer Weight Loss Surgery. The light above me shone brighter and my hunger for change grew.

Finding out about weight loss surgery was an eye opener. I hadn't expected it to sound as hard as they, the clinics, were making out. It seems that WLS has its own set of by-products and negative connotations. At this point I could smell the eye of the storm was coming to an end and sensed that the other side might be even more furious than its beginning. It was coming and there was nothing I could do. I was stuck in this eye and had two options, give in and the storm might devour me like a hungry wave, chomping and frothing towards the lighthouse, ravenous and unforgiving, like obesity had been to me. My only fear was that the waves might gather momentum and melt me away like sugar crystals in a scalding hot pan, leaving me liquefied, becoming the watery wave itself. Or I could get myself a waxed board and learn how to surf, to navigate the storm and not let the tidal surge engulf me, not let obesity have the last hurrah. I could simmer and swim instead of melting in a congealed, almost burned, syrup.

The more I researched, the brighter the light. The eye of the storm was so fast, the breakfast rush was over but the lunch time rush contained dinner as well, it was coming for me and I had to batten down my hatches and get prepared.

We couldn't afford it. It was nearly £10,000, just not possible.

Bypassing Obesity

However, the candelas from my lighthouse shone brighter. The eye of the storm grew smaller, it was coming. The positives of WLS outnumbered the negative (of which there were many). It was going to be my beginning and my end.

I just had to fund it. But how?

I am humble and grateful. I am also extremely fortunate that I have a family that have worked incredibly hard and have a successful business, almost to the detriment of family-life. I have a family that were able to help me, to ultimately save me.

I called my dad one evening and talked him through my realisation about obesity. It was a long conversation that didn't involve me asking for money but explained that I had researched WLS and that it seemed to be an option for me, a way out of the obesity trap. I told my dad that I was going to research it more thoroughly and we would talk again.

And so we did indeed talk again, at length. I had researched all manner of surgeries and had an idea of what they entailed, the success rates and by-products, side effects and safety. Any questions Dad asked me, I had a response for. Again, I didn't ask him for a handout, I was just sounding him out before I tried to get the surgery using a loan or payment plan. My dad is level-headed and practical, and so he seemed like a good person to chat to about such a huge decision. In the meantime, I decided that I'd book a private appointment to see a gastric surgery specialist at a private hospital nearby and find out more about price, recovery, and the payment plan. The private consultation was over £150 for half an hour, but I found the money and Dad said he would come with me and wanted to chat to me, my mum and husband before we went.

It was a bit like an intervention with my parents asking worried questions; asking me how I would cope with not being able to eat as I currently did, a fair question. They deeply worried that I would fall into a black hole of depression if my beloved food crutch was no longer an option to me.

I had to try and explain about how I felt in my heart and soul about being obese, and all its by-products, in a way that I'd not done before.

A gate to honesty had been swung open and I had expelled all my deepest feelings concerning my size. I had been trying to process emotionally my own fears and feelings and it felt good to finally have a frank and honest conversation with the three people who loved me most. I spoke about my addictions to foods and my panic when they were unavailable. I talked about the deepest regrets of being a morbidly obese parent. I explained the avoidance of having to go upstairs unless absolutely necessary. The way that obesity treated me as a woman, a mother, friend, and daughter. I opened up about fitting into chairs, tables and travel situations, much like I have in the previous chapters.

I had always been under a cloud of confidence and a hidden under the guise of *fat and proud*, although I did, in all honesty, feel glam and pretty as an obese woman and as I've said before I love attention and so it sometimes suited me. It was no shock for Mum and Dad to know my true feelings and learn of my revelation, but I think they were shocked at my admittance. My husband already knew the struggles and boundaries that obesity gave me, as he saw it first hand in day to day life.

Both Mum and Dad were concerned that I was considering something as drastic as a surgical route to kick obesity's arse and I guess as a parent you don't want to see your child go under the knife, particularly as being put under at such a heavy weight has a high risk associated with it. They both asked me to "give it one more shot" at a conventional diet and exercise plan, as I'm sure most people would agree with. Why not just try again?

Bypassing Obesity

My answer is this: how many times is enough? How many diets, how many new starts, how many tough love talks and failed attempts, is enough? How many times standing holding the bags whilst your family go on the rides at the fair? Or walks cut short? How many airplane seats or cinema seats should bruise my hips before it's enough to make me want it enough to really go for it "this time"?

Of course, there is no right or wrong answer and obviously it's a very individual line in the sand. Some people manage really well to escape obesity using diets and movement. Some lose weight through stress, some by hypnosis or medication. There are people I've known to lose vast amounts of weight at many periods of their lives only to re-gain. The thing with addictions is that it can lay dormant whilst you are in recovery, but it never goes away. Once you slide off the wagon it can bite back with the jaws of a ravenous beast, gaining strength whilst dormant, it feeds on failure and self-loathing and so it can escalate, bringing a hungrier addiction than before. My fear was this: in my state of mind I might have been able to lose some weight. I may have been successful enough to lose, let's say, 10% of my excess weight, but would that be forever? I wanted a forever. I wanted a route out of obesity that could give me the start that I needed but also a chance to remain in the same direction and stay at the destination. I didn't want a return ticket.

So, in September 2019 my husband, dad and I went off to Springfield Hospital to meet Mr Janthie, the bariatrics surgeon.

I was twenty-three stone and three pounds.

I was thirty-nine years old and a size 28.

I was desperate but optimistic for change.

* I want to say at this point that is in no way a story to encourage people to go out and have weight loss surgery. I'm not promoting it or endorsing it to others as a get out of jail free card. I'm simply telling my story and documenting my journey that happens to involve WLS. It's not for everyone and it's certainly not easy, physically, or mentally. It's just my story.

THIRTEEN

Autumn

Okay, let's start with some dates. Not the nice, new romance kind, the definite, actual time kind. Its 2020 and Covid has hit us all, whether it be within the vice like grasps of the physical virus, or the ripples of the bastard thing. We are all at home when we aren't at work or shopping and it's like we are living in a dystopian novel, only the novel is so far-fetched that it's well out of the ordinary realms of fiction. This is some real shit going down. It's life-altering and we're living in a bubble of fear and confinement.

What is there to do whilst we are within the confines of our homes? Well some of us had a vice, a coping mechanism. We ate. We ate and we ate, then some of us drank too. The summer was so kind, it was warm and easy. Easy to sit and bask in the beautiful heat, easy to indulge without restrictions and unconsidered judgments. The old friend visited with gusto, she gave addiction a boost and took away self-control and all reason.
You see by this season I had visited a local hospital that offers WLS and had met a surgeon, I had booked a date for my life changing surgery and underlined it.

Sarah-Jane Oakenfull

Covid had stolen it and erased the date, but it was okay because addiction was here and she was going nowhere, she'd stay with me and push me through this lockdown by keeping me locked in. I had to fight, hard, I had to fight dirty.

So, for my 40th birthday, I asked for a bike. Ever seen a forty-year-old, twenty-three stone woman in hysterical laughter riding a bike? Well it was a sight to behold. It was so fun; I'd remembered how to ride and it felt very liberating to be able to zoom away on the solid metal structure that was my ride. Heavy duty mother fucker, that bike was. The saddle not so much. Take a moment if you can to imagine all that weight on a six inch wide, hard saddle. My arse was at least a metre and a half wide. That's about 75 centimetres of flesh either side of the appendage. Yes, it was uncomfortable. No, it was actually agony after a few minutes, and it took all my might to go on bike rides in that first lockdown, but I was in battle mode by then. The battle ended up with me laying on my front on the lounge floor not being able to sit down on my fleshy bum for a good few days. Agony. On one occasion we went off with the best will in the world on a "little" bike ride and ended up going through all the small villages on a mammoth five-mile stint. *Fuck my actual life*, it was hell, but I did it.

Anyway, it was the summer of 2020, and my weight was creeping up. Although I was trying to control my eating and this new exercise/condemnation was going as well as it could, I had a niggle that my life should be changing, my mind should be changing, getting ready for the biggest change my life would ever see. Lockdown treated us all so differently that I couldn't surmise that all obese human beings suffered the same lack of control as myself, but in talking to a number of others it seems that a majority found this the case.

Bypassing Obesity

As we all did, I muddled through the pandemic in those first few months trying to navigate and normalise this new world that we found ourselves surviving in. Weight-wise I seemed to stay around 23 and a half stone but I had now reached a size 30 dress. I remember a denim oversized shirt I ordered in a size 32 so it was big and baggy to wear with leggings and a scarf. It was too tight and that really hit me hard. I hid the poxy thing in the back of the wardrobe just so as I didn't have to see it and be reminded of my size. My disappointment at myself seemed to grow from there on in. And all the while I waited for the surgery day to be rescheduled.

I used the time wisely, as in I read and researched addictions and weight loss surgery until I felt like I had a good grasp as to what I was letting myself in for and I slowly started to address food addiction, desperation to feel full and the physical need for those hyper-palatable foods, my crutches. I'm not saying for one second that I suddenly didn't have an addiction to food or feeling full, but I had stepped up and looked it squarely, seriously and sternly in the face and truly acknowledged and excepted it. That was progress indeed.

As with any addictions, they don't simply go away. If you are an addict, you're an addict for life. The recovery is for life and maintenance is crucial, just getting through the hours, days and months living in recovery. No food addict simply stops being such, we have to learn to live with binging or excesses behaviours towards food. It's bloody tough, as I've said before, we have to eat. Food addiction is complex as we can't simply stop eating, and so it can tend to create more relapses.

No weight loss surgery, diet, pills, or options can cure overeating or food addictions. Having your stomach tied, cut, bypassed, or sleeved does not cure addiction and could in fact cause a depressive pattern, as in you physically cannot eat to excess, and so the cycle of depression can roll on and on, using what's known as "slider" foods to aid the rotation. These foods are easily consumed in small amounts but have no particular nutritious value, your biscuits, crisps and such like. Many people I've spoken to have reverted back to their eating habits from pre-op days, all be it on a smaller scale. The addiction is always there, whatever the action to escape obesity. I will delve deeper into this but for now I just wanted to cement the fact that weight loss surgery can aid obesity, yes, but it cannot fix addiction or mental health issues.

The date came. In what was in a very freaky twist of fate, I was actually eating a McDonalds when a withheld number called me. The hospital that I'd visited and had been accepted by for my surgery were calling to give me another date. October the 8th 2020. it was only five weeks away.

I didn't finish my Big Mac.

A whirlwind swept through my brain.

What if it is postponed again?
Am I doing the right thing?
Will I ever enjoy food, eating again?
What if I die?

Millions of questions and worries seared through me. Concerns about the future, practicalities such as childcare and day to day living engulfed me. Who will I be if I'm no longer big, fat girl Sarah? Will my friends, particularly the ones that are obese themselves, like me and or accept me if I'm not huge? Will my husband find me attractive, will it change the dynamics within my marriage and any other relationships come to think of it?

Bypassing Obesity

Having said this, being over wrought with worries and questions, my main and most profound state of reaction was one of calm assurance and a deep acceptance that this was the exact thing I need to do. This was written somewhere within my plan, my path was set to reach this somehow. That didn't mean that I wasn't absolutely shitting myself and making plans with friends to be strong female figures for my daughters if I should die on the operating table. It was very surreal, and I've not felt so many conflicting emotions in all my life.

Some call weight loss surgery the easy option, the no hassle, no commitment, can't-be-bothered-to-try way to beat obesity. I'd be lying if I hadn't at some point thought the same. The more I researched the more that opinion diminished, and fast.

Do I refer to it now as an effective way? Yes (for me). A drastic way? Yes, most certainly. It's a way of beating obesity that is life changing and not just for a short time but for evermore. Does it require balance and commitment? Yes!!

I joined Facebook pages and groups for obesity and weight-loss stories. I read and reread books and literature on life before, during and after WLS. I felt confident that I was doing the right thing and that I was as well prepared for what was about to happen as possible.

Now before having weight loss surgery the liver needs to be reduced in size as much as possible. Many obese people have what is called fatty liver disease, exactly what it says on the tin, layers of fat covering the liver and so enlarging it. The liver is a large organ that sits over part of the stomach and so, if it is as small as it can be, it makes the tricky operation much easier and safer. This means that before the operation is performed you have to follow a strict diet in order to reduce the liver. Surgeons and hospitals all have their own types and time frames for the liver reducing diet (LRD) but there seems to be three main diets that are recommended, depending on your BMI, weight, and degree of obesity.

These include:
The Milk LRD

This is roughly (and changes from surgeon/hospital) around three pints of milk per day, two low fat yoghurts, one salty drink (Bovril / Oxo) and plenty of fluids (water).

The SlimFast LRD
Two to four SlimFast shakes a day (pre-made) and a small calorie counted meal (again changeable from service provider), one salty drink and plenty of fluids.

The Food-Based LRD
This is a low-carb, low-energy, low-fat, medium-protein diet. Again, plenty of fluids (water).

These are the main three although I have heard of others.

These diets are hardcore, but vital in the run up to surgery. I have heard of people that cheated the LRD, have had the risky anaesthetic, the surgeon has gone in and been unable to perform the operation as the liver was not at a size that was deemed safe to be moved and operated near. Imagine getting ready for surgery and expecting to wake up all ready for a new life, only to be told it wasn't possible for the surgery to go ahead.

The liver reducing diets can cause some side-effects, and very often do. If you imagine that in general the morbidly obese person is eating more than the average sized, what a shock to the system it must be for the body to suddenly survive on this "milk diet" or indeed any of the mentioned above. The list of side-effects can include, feeling light-headed, thirsty, extremely tired, changes in bowel habits, severe headaches, shaking, concentration difficulties, low mood, sleep issues and many more. Most people tend to lose weight during the LRD stage, the average timeframe is around two weeks pre-surgery to reduce the liver enough but this is changeable. Personally, I found this part almost the hardest of all. However, sticking to a strict diet to achieve an end goal was something that felt I was able to achieve. I had a reason to do it and it was a non-negotiable part of the process.

Bypassing Obesity

If you can imagine how much harder it must be to operate on a morbidly obese person, practically, having to reach over the mass of body, cut through layers of flesh to reach the site of the body on which the surgery is to be performed on, just the sheer bulk of the person on the bed, lifting and manoeuvring it.

The risks alone of being anaesthetised as a morbidly obese person is much greater than that of an average, healthy weight. Risks of DVT or deep vein thrombosis is much greater due to the diminished movement during recovery, particularly the lack of muscle movement in the legs that help massage the flow of blood from the legs to the heart causing clots that can then travel to other areas, i.e. heart or lungs. This means a course of self-injected thinners for around ten days post-surgery to diminish the risks of clotting. There can be breathing difficulties due to the extra tissue around the neck and chest. This can make it less easy to breathe normally when under an anaesthetic. Having a high BMI means that the heart has to work much harder and so being under can contribute to a low oxygen level, as the heart is working even harder than that of an average sized individual.

There are many more risks of being morbidly obese and having an anaesthetic, of course the main one being death, quite literally.

Recovery can be much longer and that can even come down to the small external wounds from the keyhole surgery, never mind the total rearrangement and partial removal of some of the internal organs. You are encouraged to move as soon as possible after surgery to help with the risks of DVT. This can be tricky as pain relief can be another problem in an obese body, the levels or doses can vary greatly and so some might struggle more than others. Even finding a vein for a cannula can be harder. Carrying around the bulk and sheer weight of the morbid obese body after such an epic surgery is extremely hard, as I have stated before. Any movement in such a huge body is like wading through water and so when you are in pain or discomfort, and groggy after being anaesthetised, this can be bound in difficulty. These are just some of the practical, physical parts of weight loss surgery and I'd say that this is most probably around 70% of the overall experience. The other 30% is emotion and psychological adjustment at this point.

Easy right?

There are many different types of weight-loss surgery but there seems to be three main, more widely known procedures:

The Gastric Band
A surgical band is wrapped around part of the stomach to temporarily restrict the size, allowing the person to feel full on a smaller amount of food. Not usually suitable for the morbidly obese.

The Gastric Sleeve (sleeve gastrectomy)
This is a permanent, bigger operation in which part of the stomach is removed so you cannot eat as much therefore feeling fuller sooner.

The Gastric Bypass
This is when the top part of the stomach is joined to the small intestine so you feel fuller and do not absorb as many calories, or nutrients, this is also permanent.

All of these have risks and are not a quick fix and need very careful consideration.

Bypassing Obesity

With all this and a lot more besides jumbling around in my brain, I was going to do this. I had a date and so my journey began to feel very real and very imminent.

FOURTEEN

Bypassing my obesity

The date is September the 24th 2021. Today I start my liver reducing diet. I have opted for the SlimFast diet. Day one is tough but I'm running on adrenalin and excitement and very little else. I've had two ready-made shakes and a small bowl of rice and vegetables. It's okay so far. I'm hungry, but it's totally doable. I go to bed and manage to sleep pretty well. I wake on the second day feeling uneasy. My body is achy and empty. My mind is whirring and feels like it's on a spin cycle. My tummy is screaming at me the same way a toddler screams for its sandwiches to be cut into triangles instead of squares. My tummy was having a huge tantrum and my mind was in cahoots with it.

I remember rolling out of bed and heaving my body up, heavy, and weary. My head felt like it was in a vice, being squashed like cheap timber at a builder's yard. The pain soared through my brian like a jack hammer. I burst into tears.

I did not stop crying for very long on that second day. It was as if something or someone had died and I was grieving and in a way that's exactly what I was doing. I was in mourning, for food, for sugar and fats. The next twelve days felt like decades in my fuzzed head.

Sarah-Jane Oakenfull

I didn't get dressed that day. I sat in my pyjamas and a scruffy headband, old slippers, and my daughter's duvet across me, sat on the sofa. I didn't even brush my teeth. I sat all greasy and stinking, feeling incredibly sorry for myself, in deep, deep grief. A black hole. Only there was a very tiny pin of light, the light was twelve days away and I had to grow that pin head into a ray of light and let it grow in order to open the shutters and let the full blaze of light through. So somehow I got through the day and ended up bathing, and after watching crap TV and my husband looking after the kids solo, me just soaking up some TLC, I went to bed a bit easier.

The next day was much, much better and the school run beckoned, so I really had no option but to get up and get on. Every day after that it got a little bit easier, although my tummy screamed out loud like a banshee for all to hear and the hunger, addiction was very real. It was easier until on the eleventh night it was almost okay. Very much achieved and I felt very proud of myself: I hadn't cheated, not even once. Even when I went to my brother's and he and his family had Domino's pizza and invited us to stay, I simply sat in the lounge whilst the rest of the clan, including my children, indulged.

How did I sleep that night, the night before it all began? Well quite simply, I didn't really. However, I figured that I'd be put out into my unconscious anaesthetic soon so I didn't have much use for sleep. I had done two weeks of LRD and was feeling pretty fucking special and proud to be honest.

Bearing in mind that at this time we were deep in the throes of a global pandemic, the restrictions around hospitals were still very tight. I had to self-isolate for a week before and week after my surgery date. This meant that my husband had to have two weeks off work and the girls would have to have a fortnight off school. Or, my chosen option, I stayed at my mum's, and she went to stay with my brother.

Bypassing Obesity

So, the week before my operation I was alone in my mum's one bedroomed bungalow. Living within a bubble of facetime and loneliness, I binged Netflix. *Orange is the New Black* was devoured like a chocolate egg at easter. I had some crazy dreams that week, what with all my emotions and the dark, witty prison drama.

The night before it all began, I sat alone, ate my microwave, calorie-counted meal and had a few grapes as a treat and went to bed for a sleepless rest.

The next morning when I decided it was an acceptable time to rise, I showered. My mum's shower is in a tiny bathroom with no bath, just a stand-in small shower with a narrow sliding door. It had been a struggle to get in all week but this morning the action of squeezing in sideways made me grin through my nerves. An excitement came over me as I squashed the hanging flabby rolls through the narrow door. This was it, the time has come and I'm ready. I'm also absolutely fucking shitting myself.

I put on some gospel music, my go-to in difficult times and tried to relax. I couldn't sit still not even for a second. I went through my bags again to check I had everything I needed. I had purchased some new luggage for my first stay in a private hospital just in case anyone saw through me and realised I didn't actually belong there. I had a large holdall with a matching bag in a calming blue colour with bees on. A Sophie Allport bee bag and some emphasis on my "T's" and no one need know I was a poor council chick pretending to be posh at this private gaff.

I heard a car pull up outside and an electric shock seared through me in a frozen nanosecond. He was here to collect me and I'm so terrified yet excited I thought I might burst. My overwhelming emotion was fear, fear of not making it through the operation and leaving my girls without their mum. However, I must have sensed deep down that this was extremely unlikely as I got up and grabbed my bags and coat and I walked out to the car on the start of my journey.

Sarah-Jane Oakenfull

I had decided to try and look smart for the arrival at hospital and so I'd gone for some dark jeans, a smart black shirt and a scarf that matched my luggage, topped off with a smart black wool coat.

I got into the car with my husband, and we drove the twenty-minute car ride, making jokes and trying to make light of this weird situation. He did ask me if I was sure that I wanted to go through with it and I replied without hesitation, "Yes".

When we arrived at the main entrance of the hospital a porter met me at the door. There was a very strict No Visitor policy due to Covid, so I was to walk in alone. I kissed my husband and told him I loved him, picked up my posh new luggage and walked in. I had my temperature checked and signed a form to say I hadn't had any symptoms of Covid and followed the man through to the ward. I looked back in time to see Chris driving away. I was alone in a hospital of strangers in an unfamiliar environment, having major surgery. I did have nice luggage though.

My body was shaking and my armour of humour came to join me. I kept making some pretty pathetic jokes that I can't remember (frozen out of my mind). I have never felt so many emotions in my life. Scared, excited, terrified, calm, sure, guilty, just a huge bundle of emotions all mixed into one mind.

A kindly nurse met us at the doors of the ward and introduced herself. She was a bit older than me, maybe fifty, blond hair tied back in a low ponytail. She was just slightly larger than average and when I made some more stupid jokes, she said she understood and she was doing Slimming World at the moment. I didn't think she needed to, she looked fabulous to me.

Bypassing Obesity

She took me to my room, number one (always). It was as posh as I had imagined and again I made a joke about it being like a hotel and I'm only here for a break. The room had a large flat screen TV on the wall, pictures over the bed. There was a little bag of mini cosmetics on some fluffy folded towels on the bed. The room had a large window with views of a small garden. There was a small wardrobe and a chair that in days of past had most probably been used by loved ones visiting. Now it housed only my luggage. The bathroom was bigger than mine at home and had a large mirror with a light behind it. The shower was huge and looked like it might double up as a massager, it had such a large head on it. The sink had a vanity unit and even a small glass over the top of a paper doily, like in hotels.

Now I like a bit of posh and although I did feel like an imposter, I strangely felt right at home too.

The room was calm, clean, and homely and I felt a bit more relaxed as I looked around. I unpacked my cosmetics in the bathroom and took out my slippers and dressing gown and laid them on the bed. The lovely nurse came back and I had to fill in and sign some paper work. She told me I was first in today and said to get changed into the gown, ready for my operation.

I was alone. I changed and took a few selfies, as you do. I decided not to tell my parents or Chris that I was going in first or they might worry whilst waiting to hear from me. I called Helen. I made her promise that she'd look after Chris and the girls if I died, and she laughed and promised me she would. We had a giggle about the food menu and what a waste it was to be in a posh private hospital and not be able to take full advantage of the offering. We said goodbye and I told her I'd call when I could.
Mum had written me a card to take to hospital and so I opened it and read some beautiful words of love and encouragement, telling me what a strong woman I was, and I was, she was right. It had a blessing written in the card too and I held onto it with all my soul. I had taken a photo of the girls with me and put it and the card from Mum on the windowsill so that I could see it from the bed.

All of my best friends sent me messages and my dear family all contacted me to give their support and love. I felt very special and important. I felt so much love and I knew I was doing the right thing.

I text Chris and said I loved him and the girls, and laid on the bed not expecting to sleep but hoping to get some rest.

A knock at the door made me jump out of my skin. My nurse came in and said they were ready for me. The surgical ward was opposite the nurses' station right next to my room and the nurse said to come out and walk across. Suddenly I felt very alone. I asked if she would come with me, she of course agreed. Like a child I grabbed her hand, and we walked in the pre-op room hand in hand. She passed me over to the team, ready with the anaesthetist and others, I wasn't quite sure of their roles. I climbed on the bed, again making a joke about it holding me, and they asked me some questions and explained exactly what was going to happen, all very polite and easy. They were kind and could see my shaking body. As they started to insert the anaesthetic I said "Please don't let me die," to which they said that wouldn't happen, and through my slitted eyelids I remember the team smiling.

FIFTEEN

Obesity bypassed

I'm awake. It's black. I'm asleep, but not the all-out anaesthetised sleep but the aftereffects of it. It's completely black and my eyes, my mind, cannot open enough to be fully conscious. I can feel a strange sensation on my calves, tightening, release, tightening, release, almost like a blood pressure cuff only it's on my lower legs.

Asleep, awake, semi-conscious. Tightening, release. I feel so warm it's like I'm in a cocoon, warm and safe and dark. My eyes won't open and I think I made a soft moaning noise at the tightening of whatever was happening to my legs. Briefly I wondered if maybe I had something wrong with me and they had operated on them, then more sleep.

Awake again, so warm and feeling so comforted by the warmth and the heaviness of my sleepy state. I manage to raise an eyelid this time and see a nurse. I smile and felt my eyes roll in my head, but softly like a floating bubble. The nurse had dark hair and beautiful dark eyes and was smiling at me, greeting me with a toothy smile. I think she was talking but I've no idea what she's saying, I'm so tired and warm. Tightening again, then release. The nurse does my observations and tells me that the surgery went really well and they had put a special blanket on me as my temperature was slightly low. Okay, so that explains the warmth.

I try to talk but my throat is so dry that it's a crackle more than a sentence. I need to let Chris know I'm alive and my girls will be worried. The nurse seems to have mind-reading abilities and offers me a sip of water. That water was like the actual nectar of the gods, and it almost felt like oiling a rusty hinge. "Please may I call my husband?" I manage. I looked over at my card from Mum and the picture of my girls and smiled, then I fell asleep again.

I can't tell you how many times I went back to sleep or when I found out that the sensation on my calves was actually a device that stimulates the muscles to prevent blood clots and DVTs. I'd also love to compare the cocooned feeling to emerging, from caterpillar to a beautiful wing-spreading creature, but laying in that bed all warm and snug, I was more like a slug!

I did manage to call Chris and most probably sounded like I'd had a skin full of cheap cider on the verge of alcohol induced illness. I only said a few words and one of those was a swear. I told him I'd call when I was awake. Like actually awake and not in an anaesthetic daze.

I must admit I had no pain at all at this point and felt only comfort and warmth, just remembering it now is making me feel all fuzzy. Here I was, an obese mum of two from a council estate, in a private hospital, wrapped up like a newborn baby in a timeless bundle.

The next few hours were a blur of sleep and moments of semi-consciousness. I can't remember what the timeframe was when I began to feel human enough to sit up and take the first few steps to the bathroom. I managed to call Chris that evening and have a conversation and told him to call my parents and Helen for me, as I was too tired. I used the huge flat screen TV and watched some TV, a gangster movie if memory serves.

Bypassing Obesity

During the night the nurses came in and did my observations every few hours. I was encouraged to have sips of water every hour and tried my best, but the tiredness engulfed me. The leg tighteners came off, replaced with the god-awful stockings that restrict the blood flow and feel like they are strangling your chubby legs. It took some time for the poor nurse to get them on and she had to go to find the biggest size they had. Even those were too tight and rolled down. Eventually they had to be removed as they really did restrict the blood flow. When they took them off it was similar to having had an upset tummy and trying to keep it in, then eventually getting to the loo. The relief was immense.

After a good night's sleep, more sleep and plenty of pain killers, I felt vaguely human the next morning. I managed to get up and have a shower. I pulled the emergency cord in the bathroom as I could see drops of blood dripping down onto the floor. That troubled me greatly and I burst into tears. Turned out it was from my tiny puncture wound that my blood thinning injection had made and was very insignificant indeed. I felt like a right tit as two nurses ran, in followed by my surgeon, me standing stark bollock naked, crying like a bitch. I had five large dressings on my vast tummy, the entry points for the surgery. One roughly above my belly button, one centre right of that and two centre left, then one under my left breast. It was quite a sight to behold, all bruised and dressed up, my large tummy consisted of two rolls, one upper hanging mass and one hanging lower under where my bellybutton is. All of the entry points were to the upper section of my tummy, and I wasn't able to wear a bra at first, as it rubbed on my incision.

I had my breakfast, this was a cup of coffee (*aaahhhhh*, it was incredible), and a pot of orange jelly of which I managed one and a half mouthfuls. At this point I'll tell you it was a Saturday and the only television programs available to me were mainly cooking related programming. Bit of a low blow given the circumstances.

Sarah-Jane Oakenfull

I sat up in the comfy grey chair for a bit and tiredness hit me again and so I laid back in the bed and had another sleep. When I woke up for my obs and painkillers, I sat up and facetimed my husband and the girls. They seemed more interested in the posh hospital room than how I was feeling. I managed to stay awake long enough to call both my parents and Helen. I was encouraged to get up and go for a walk. Although my pain was in control, I did feel timid and fragile, afraid to overdo it in case I did some internal damage. Also, the absolute tiredness and pure exhaustion from the anaesthetic was overwhelming, so I napped on and off all day. That evening, I got up and went for a walk into the little garden. I'm not gonna lie, I went out to have a vape. I called my precious Nana and had a lovely chat, I let her know I was okay, and she was glad to hear from me. My Nana has struggled with her weight since I can remember, and she has always been concerned for me, as well as sympathetic.

I had the most wonderful experience in the hospital and could not fault the care I was given. To be honest I didn't want to go home. I was having a few mouthfuls of jelly and cups of tea; they encouraged me to drink (sip) water regularly. All my medication was crushed up and put into tiny cups of water. I think this was the worst bit about the whole ordeal, it tasted absolutely vile. The painkillers I had been on for the first 12 or so hours had been reduced to simple liquid paracetamol, and I had that every four hours. I was doing really well, and it was suggested that I could go home. However the thought of going back to Mum's bungalow by myself didn't appeal to me at all and I was enjoying being looked after in such a posh manner. I said that I'd be ready to go home tomorrow, and they said that'd be fine. If I'm honest I'd have stayed a bloody week if I could have.

That night I slept very well again and by the morning I was moving much easier. Although there was discomfort and it felt very much like I'd had an operation, it was okay. The pain was manageable and, other than the lingering tiredness and the absence of food, I was feeling good.

Bypassing Obesity

By this stage I had not seen Chris since about 7:30, Friday morning when he dropped me at the hospital doors. We had spoken and facetimed but it's just not the same as seeing someone in the flesh, particularly after going through such a huge surgery.

I had got myself a new lounge wear suit to wear in hospital but as I'd been so tired I had stayed in my night dress and pyjamas the entire stay, so the morning I was going home I decided I'd better put on something that resembled clothes. The new lounge wear was a top and trouser combo in light cream. It was really soft and comfortable. I'd gotten it from an online catalogue called Simply Be and it was a size twenty-eight. I wanted something that fitted nicely under my surgery points and the trousers fit really well. I'd lost a stone on the LRD diet, so a size twenty-eight was perfect by then.

So braless but in my new loungewear, I waited for Chris to call and let me know he was outside. I had the nurse talk me through my medication and cover exactly what liquids I was able to have. She told me again and again the importance to having plenty of fluids, sip, sip, sip, sip being the mantra. I was shuffling around packing my posh bags up, laughing at myself for being such a dickhead about luggage and realising it had made not one sodding difference to me or anyone else what luggage I had came with.

My phone buzzed and I felt a bolt of electric course through me as it signalled Chris was here to collect me. My nurse carried my posh luggage for me to the main entrance of the hospital and handed me over to Chris, who looked very relieved to see me but seemed a bit hesitant to hug me. He put the posh bags in the boot and helped me get into the car. The nurse then explained to him about my oral pain relief and again the importance of sipping liquids regularly. He thanked her, as did I and we were away.

I was so pleased to be with him and be going back to Mum's for a week before going home but I suddenly felt tearful. Chris was talking about the girls and what they'd be up to, having a moan about their bedrooms, all the usual shit that goes with family life.

It suddenly struck me that I'd just had a massive life-changing operation and the life I was driving back to was not the same life I'd driven away from. Also, I was completely in charge of the rest of this journey.

It was now up to me to do the work; the surgery had gone really well but that was just the beginning. Here is where it starts, right here, right now. I was alone to do my bit, it was completely up to me now. Also, the journey wasn't comfortable on my tummy and the very real feeling that my insides had been moved was apparent. The seat belt was tight and very much unsuitably situated for where my incisions were.

Chris noticed I was upset and asked if I was in pain and so I just said yes and we drove home in a bit of a sombre mood. Until he asked me if I wanted a KFC then we both laughed and I said I'd prefer a Burger King or McDonald's. We had such a laugh about all the cookery programs on the TV at the weekend and he asked if I felt hungry, did I feel different? In truth I didn't feel hungry, just a bit strange. You see, when most of your waking hours are taken up by the thought of food or cravings for certain foods, it's a strange feeling to then know that you're not able to have any solid food at all. It wasn't an awful, desperate feeling, I think I was as prepared as I could have been mentally. However it was a very definite feeling, and I could have easily been consumed by it.

I put on a positive voice of reason and kept thinking of the future and how it would look, and more importantly feel, to be smaller and able-bodied. I kept thinking about how wonderful it would be to run, climb, play, and live without morbid obesity. Even in those first few days I had to give myself a talking-to and remind myself why I had done this and look ahead. "Just keep swimming," as Dory would say.

SIXTEEN

Support in a "C" cup

Support comes in many forms. A good, firm support bra, for instance is a crucial part of an obese woman's attire. No such thing as a C cup in my obese life, I was a 44 H in the boulder holder department at my heaviest. I do however have a C in my life that is perhaps my biggest support, even bigger than my sturdiest bra, and that support is Chris.

I didn't really even realise how much I needed him until the first few days post-op. I had been deposited back at my mum's little bungalow, alone again. Although I did end up calling Mum to come and stay with me. I should mention that my grandad had very recently died, and it was two days before his funeral, so my mum was feeling very emotional, bless her. I think coming home to look after me was a bit of a distraction from her grief, very briefly. Chris had gone home to look after the girls, and I'd said a tearful goodbye to him and we said we'd talk later that evening. He had come in to Mum's with me and made me a cup of tea and taken the posh luggage in, made sure I was set up with everything I needed.

Mum and I sat and watched TV that evening and I spent a while calling with Chris and the girls. I still felt exhausted and went to bed in Mum's single bed, propped up by six pillows, as it hurt to lay flat. I had taken my painkillers regularly, a duo of soluble co-codamol and liquid ibuprofen. I slept really well and tried to keep sipping water, but I felt so full so quickly, and it made me feel very sick.

The next morning Chris took the girls to school and arrived at Mum's door with bags of shopping. He had brought all manner of ingredients with him and set about batch cooking numerous soups for me. He got very bossy about my fluid intake and set a five-minute timer to encourage me to drink. He cooked up a storm and made me roasted garlic and butternut squash, leek and potato, stilton and broccoli soups and divided them out into tiny Tupperware pots he had gotten from the shop that morning. He helped me into the shower and dried my hair for me. He helped me walk around the bungalow and made me hot water bottles.

My husband is a good man, but… he is not one for pandering, sympathy doesn't come naturally to him. Whenever I've been poorly, he's not been the most patient nurse. He was wonderful when we had the miscarriages and you couldn't want for a better birthing partner, but sick bugs, viruses and infections are not in his realms of compassion. I didn't really know what to expect from him, support-wise after the surgery. I knew he would be kind as he was one hundred percent behind my decision to have bariatric surgery, but I did wonder how patient he'd be after. He's a very practical man, also very black and white. With Chris there is no grey area.

Bypassing Obesity

He spent an hour or so with me after the soup making and sat and watched me consume some. I say watched, he sat and lectured me until I'd had at least three spoonfuls, then sat for half an hour until I could drink, just to make sure I did just that. He then had to pop to work before collecting the girls from school. He brought the girls to see me on the doorstep of the bungalow after school, but we all found it incredibly hard as I was self-isolating. I shouldn't risk hugging them after they had been at school and potentially exposed to Covid. I think you all know what happened. I held my children close. So sue me.

Another evening for Mum and I to sit and chat about life. This was the night before Grandpa's funeral so we looked at old pictures and talked about his days as a cowboy in Canada. We talked about how Pa would've been very really pleased that I'd had the surgery and what a shame he'd never see the end result. We both had a broken night's sleep, poor Mum on the sofa feeling very emotional and uncomfortable.

Mum woke early and my brother picked her up ready to travel to Pa's funeral. I did feel horribly guilty about not being able to attend but at the same time I was in more pain in those few days after surgery than I had been the immediately after. I'm pretty sure Grandpa would have been content for me to stay home and sing a few bars for him instead so that's exactly what I did.

Mum was obviously gone all day into the late evening but towards the afternoon, Chris popped by with the girls. He didn't come in with them, but we stood on the doorstep for a while. When he started to leave, I must have looked a bit sad and so he came into the bungalow and sat me in the armchair. He made me a cup of tea and stayed for a while longer. I couldn't put my finger on what I was feeling, maybe some sort of post-operation blues, or the aftereffects of an anaesthetic, or perhaps the funeral of my Grandpa Music, but a deep sadness came over me when he went to leave again. I tried not to show it. By this time the girls were bored of seeing Mum and the novelty of it all had well and truly worn off, so they were being, as children are, a bit twattish.

Sarah-Jane Oakenfull

They left and I sat feeling sorry for myself. The world felt incredibly big, and I felt very alone. I had a yearning to be with Chris and only Chris. It wasn't a loneliness I'd experienced before. We've been apart for separate holidays with mates and the odd few days but never in a situation where one of us was ill or in discomfort. I wanted him. I wanted to be held by him and I think even if Tom Hardy or Chris Pratt walked in, I'd have still just wanted 'my' Chris. When he got home, he called me.

We live about ten minutes from Mum's bungalow, and he had driven home and started the girls dinner. I burst into tears at the sound of his voice and he immediately said he would come back. I told him I was fine, just being silly and over-emotional. We chatted for a bit and I told him I was much better for our chat. Mum's doorbell rang and I heaved myself up to answer it and there stood my husband. Hot tears for no particular reason dribbled down my chubby face and he simply wiped them away and held me. More tea, more bossy water reminders, a shower was suggested and then soup was heated, consumed and the kitchen cleaned. The kids had been threatened to behave so sat watching TV while we just sat holding hands until my intervention from Chris was done. He left and this time I felt more content and a bit happier than the previous goodbye.

A few days bumbled past and I drank intermittently. I managed to have some soup, roughly four spoonful's a few times a day. I even managed to sip on some slim fast shakes too, a meal replacement. I was having to take the painkillers regularly and in turn I had to take a laxative, as they can make you constipated. Along with the low fluid intake, next to nothing to sustain me, it got to about day six post-op and I still hadn't been to the toilet. I hadn't shit for almost a week.

If you've ever had constipation, like proper hard, childbirth-type constipation then I know you'll understand this next paragraph. And if you haven't then, well, never let yourself become clogged up to the point of grade three tearing/caesarean evacuation. When they tell you to keep up your fluids then fucking well do it! I had some seepage. Overflow.

Bypassing Obesity

Basically I had a massive hard poo stuck somewhere between my bowels and my arse hole and if I hadn't known what it was like to sit on an oak log, I do now. The pain was actually eye-watering. The small amount of liquefied faeces that could manoeuvre around the hard lump was coming out at involuntary intervals. The pain was making me feel very unwell. The pain from the huge surgery I'd had was made worse by the constipation and the actual pain in my arse was like pulling a concrete Christmas cracker up the bum.

Honestly the memory of trying, for two whole days, to pass that solid mass of excrement is something I've tried very hard to forget but it is, in fact etched into my brain, possibly as a stark reminder to fucking drink more.

I lay on my mother's sofa, on a large towel, knickers-less, on my side (which in itself was very uncomfortable due to said surgery), liquid faecal matter oozing from my bum, crying because I couldn't sit on my big bum, weight pushing down on the solid log. I sat on the toilet for an hour at a time not wanting to strain too hard and damage my inside or rip open my arsehole. I had my Mum getting warm jugs of water and pouring them down the bottom of my back while I lent forwards on the toilet, just to trying and soothe my wretched rectum. When the time came for me to birth this 2lb 6oz substantial sprog of a turd, I swear to God I nearly hit my head on the ceiling I shot up so high. The pain, followed by the absolute and definite relief, was so gratifying that I did briefly wonder if I was a subconscious BDSM fan for a split second.

Anyway, that took a turn, trying to explain my support system and husband, and ending up talking all about bottoms, poo, and constipation. Coincidence?

Sarah-Jane Oakenfull

I was in a bad way, emotionally, I hadn't slept for two days with the constipation and the pain from my operation was niggling still. I wanted my home, my bed and most of all my husband. Mum was absolutely brilliant; she fussed about me and took brilliant care of me but Chris knew I needed to be bossed about and taken care of in a different way. I, in absolutely NO WAY mean a sexual one, I just needed Chris. He arrived after dropping the girls at school without me asking or any actual words spoken about it and told me he was taking me home.

Isn't it funny what we take for granted? I've moaned quite a lot about Chris' inability to be sympathetic and compassionate, his way of being so black and white and not being over-emotional and now here I was craving it like a bacon sandwich after a heavy night. He was exactly what I needed, his straight-talking, no-nonsense approach to life at the exact moment was what got me through and ultimately spurred me on and kept me going. Sometimes in any relationship, but particularly in a marriage, the daily routine and mundane grind can overshadow the grass roots of what it is that makes us love someone. I know that within my own marriage, I take the small things for granted and usually Chris pisses me off with his bluntness so when I realised that it was the very thing I needed from him, it took me by surprise. When the chips are down, look for your salt and vinegar, Chris is mine.

In 1994, I had a group of mates from the local area. We all went to the same school and one of the lads had a brother in the year below. An irritating little shit, a bit like a puppy, eager to please and 'fit in' with us older ones. The sibling and I were often late to school and ended up walking together sometimes. He had terrible acne, was short and, like I said, he was really bloody irritating. Absolutely no spark of attraction there at all for me at that time.

Bypassing Obesity

Fast forward a few years and a few of us were in shared houses or homeless hostels in the same town. Teenagers whose parents had had enough or vice versa and ended up without a fixed abode could house share with the support of a housing officer (usually a hippy or kindly older lady, sometimes a scary one). That's where I was at the time. I won't go into it too much, but the teenage years had been unkind to me, and I'd lived with both parents and just not seemed to be wanted, if I'm completely honest. I wasn't a particularly difficult girl. Gobby, yes. Loud and argumentative, yes. I did make certain situations very difficult. But no child should ever be left to feel like they are unwanted by their parents. I'll leave that there as my parents are all a huge support and provide me unconditional love these days. I was the eldest child in our family and that's all I'll say.

Anyway, I was eighteen and living in a shared house as was Chris' brother, in a house around the corner and we often all got together. I don't know how or when, but we seemed to get on well and ended up starting a friendship that lasted years, like best friends. We shared a bed, and nothing happened for years. We had some really good times, full of laughter and everyone assumed we were together. I assumed he was gay, not because he hadn't made any moves, I'm not that fond of myself.

After a few other very brief 'relationships', AKA encounters, for both parties' sides, I started to have feelings for this irritating brother of my mates. He became very attractive and funny, kind and generous. He had a job and would get me a naan bread every Thursday when he was paid. He'd turn up with bits of groceries or a CD for me. We really were best mates, but I'd been hiding these increased feelings I was having for him. Without warning I had become deeply in love. It was a very gradual and intense emotion that consumed me. I lived alongside Chris as best friends for several years before we got together, his whole cheeky, irritant vibe, evolved into a stronger, head strong and outspoken one and this appealed to me greatly.

One of the great things about falling in love with your best friend is that they have seen you at your very best and your absolute worst. He had seen in in my underwear getting ready for nights out, and he had seen me in my undies after a night out with sick dried in my hair. So, although it was strange to share the intimate and romantic sides of ourselves, I never felt ashamed of my rolls, lumps and bumps as he had seen them all before. He had never made me feel unattractive, ever. Although he is not a gushy, complimentary man he has always subtly made me feel like I am good enough. He has however in more recent years addressed the health indications that being obese caused potentially. It always ended in me crying guilty tears, him getting cross that I'd taken it the wrong way and, after a while, brushing away the elephant in the room. Sometimes he would suggest that we both try a new healthy living plan, and that would always end in tears too.

When I voiced my intentions regarding weight loss surgery, there was no dramatic surprise, there was no an overzealous encouragement nor any clearly defined discouragement. Chris simply listened and his response was, "This has to be your decision." He was very clear about that but said that he would support me in whatever I decided to do in life. But, as he had tried to address before and met with tears and failure, he was deeply concerned about my health and ultimately how hard my life was and would worsen with age.

I had the support, both emotionally and physically that I needed from my chosen life partner. I knew I could do it, but I'd do it better with him by my side. Support is not just a firm bra, support is solid friendship based on love.

Obesity diminishing

The first few weeks after my bypass were, I'm not going to lie, tough.

Bypassing Obesity

It was uncomfortable and although being home was really wonderful, it didn't come without its difficulties too. I was bored stiff being at home not doing much at all. However big I have been, I have always been as active as possible. It felt like however much I tried to look for the future, it was hard to do so. I was on a liquid-only diet and husband made me some absolutely scrumptious soups, but I missed and longed for crunch and texture.

What I craved for most, surprisingly, was fruit. It was much more of an emotional thing than a physical one: the fact that I couldn't have any 'food' was getting harder each day rather than easier like the LRD. I started to feel like I'd never eat solid food again, although it was only for two weeks it felt like two months. We did get a juicer about ten days in, just so that I could have some fruit. Also the thought of getting constipated again terrified me, so I felt like the most natural thing to do was get some fresh foods in me and juicing seemed like the perfect thing.

It did work, thank heavens. I sipped on a glass of freshly squeezed fruit every evening and that really helped. We also made some ice pops; the crunch was satisfying and ultimately it was all extra fluids that I knew I needed. I had got myself a cute little teacup and saucer from the charity shop. It was just big enough for a cup of tea and small enough for me to finish it.

I started knitting and made a nine-inch bright yellow, triangle scarf with some impressive holes in it. It kept my mind and hands busy rather than thinking about eating and foods. Basically I was a nana for those two weeks and didn't really go out much at all. I was healing well and my incisions were almost scars, still red and itchy but all was going well, physically.

I had so much support and encouragement from friends and family. Flowers were delivered daily, and I had lots of cards. My closest mates called me every day and asked how I was. Of course Helen came round every other day, and I saw my sister-in-law loads. Then came my youngest daughter's birthday and she wanted a Chinese meal. I dreaded it to be honest, however it wasn't as bad as I'd anticipated and I had some chicken and sweetcorn soup, strained through a sieve. My god it tasted incredible, salty and tasty; I didn't really feel like I was missing out at all. Over the next few days, I got out the sewing machine and made some cushion covers and other random bits. I'm not crafty at all so they were all shit, but it kept me busy.

Things were going as well as they could go really, apart from the emotional adjustments but I was learning fast how to deal with them. One afternoon whilst my husband was out, I had a niggling tummy ache, not immense pain but enough of an uncomfortable feeling to warrant a hot water bottle and some codeine. The pain seemed to worsen and by the time my sister-in-law and my mum brought the kids back from a playdate I was in tears. They called my husband back from work and he called the ward of the private hospital to which they suggested going to the local emergency ward. There are things that can go wrong with any surgery and weight loss is no exception. My husband ran me over to A & E but he wasn't allowed in due to Covid restrictions. Once again I was alone and this time I was sat in a wheelchair in a busy emergency department, in a fair bit of pain absolutely shitting myself.

They gave me some oramorph, and I sat in that wheelchair for four or five hours before I was seen. All of a sudden, my surgeon appeared, and I felt a rush of relief flood over me. Within thirty minutes I had had a CT scan and was on a ward in a side room. They put me on a drip to be sure I wasn't dehydrated and kept on top of my pain relief.

Bypassing Obesity

Feeling much more settled and with the new knowledge that everything operation-wise was looking just fine, I did relax and manage to get some sleep. Tiredness is something that seems to be a running theme after WLS, possibly the lack of nutrition and calories? They found absolutely nothing wrong at all, which was really great, however I still had the pain, although it was manageable now.

After two nights away from my family I was allowed home and my husband picked me up and looked after me once more. It was almost time to move onto the pureed food stage and I was incredibly nervous about it after the painful episode. Just a day or two before the new food stage progressed, the pain returned and however much I'd been reassured by the scans and tests, it was very uncomfortable. I called the GP and they sent me straight back to A&E.

It was the week of my fifteenth wedding anniversary and here I was alone again, no visitors were permitted, and my telephone signal was shocking. So here I was once more, alone, wishing I could be anywhere on earth, anywhere with my husband. I spent another three days in hospital, more tests, and another CT scan, with this strange stuff you have to drink beforehand, blood tests and samples showed absolutely nothing that could cause this pain. At one point I thought they were thinking I was imagining it altogether. The pain eased off as it had done before and I was again, sent home.

Now knowing that everything was 100% fine I just accepted that maybe this pain was a blip in my recovery and within a few days of being home it eased away completely. I felt a bit of a fraud to be honest and we never did find out what the pain was.

So now with the pain gone and some sort of reality and routine kicking in we can move on the puree stage.

Sarah-Jane Oakenfull

Basically, it was baby food, the kind of mushed up vomit-looking crap you'd give a six-month-old. My first meal was so exciting with just a hint of fear. I had mashed potato with some cheese in it and some tinned tomatoes mushed up separately. Honestly it was so fucking tasty. I'd not had anything other than SlimFast, juice or soup for over two weeks and this was like Christmas dinner to me. At first it was great being able to have a wider range of foods but after the first few days it became gruelling.

One Sunday the family had a roast, just a chicken, nothing too flash but my husband is a fantastic chef and it looked like the kind of dinner I would have had second and third helpings of pre-surgery. I couldn't sit with or in fact near them, my tiny plate of baby food was depressing.

It was the first and most definitely the worst day I've had to date. I stood in our kitchen and wept. I wondered what on earth I'd done to myself and how the hell I was going to cope for the rest of my life, living without a full meal.

I went to bed that night not feeling much better but woke in the morning with a fresh perspective, particularly after I had had my weekly weigh-in at home. I had already lost two stone since the start of my LRD and seemed to be losing an average of half a stone per week. This meant I was almost out of the twenty something weight bracket and heading towards a personal goal of under twenty stones. I was twenty-one stone and one pound to be accurate and that felt incredible.

By now it was well and truly winter, and I could notice my coat was fitting a lot better. From the outside I didn't appear any different at all. I think when you are as big as I was it takes a lot for your body shape to change, for the changes to be noticeable to the outside observer. I did something I'd never dared to do before. I ordered a pair of trousers in a size twenty, red, tartan trousers. I had a pair when I was a teenager and I'd always wanted another pair and so now I finally felt like that might be achievable. When they came, I got them halfway up my thighs. I was really chuffed with that as I'd been in a size thirty for so long that the thought of a twenty had seemed like an impossible dream.

Bypassing Obesity

Slowly but surely things were changing for me, I started to notice subtle, small things were just a bit easier, by the time I had reached the under-twenty-stone mark. It was liberating. By Christmas I was able to borrow one of my mum's jumpers, a size twenty-four, that she had got large to wear with leggings. It had *Calories Don't Count at Christmas* on it in a glittery scroll. I had found a pair of jeggings in the charity shop in a size twenty-four that fit me like a glove. It was so emotional that I shed real, fat tears.

My diet was also changing, and I was able to eat a meal, like proper solid food. I still ate too quickly, old habits and all that. I was, and still am, sick and get what's called the 'foamies' if I eat too quickly or too much.

As my tummy is smaller it no longer has the same amount of bile to help break down the food, so if I don't chew well enough, or if I eat too much, my tummy produces a foam like substance that forms and makes its way up to be expelled along with small amounts of the foods consumed. This often, for me comes with a horrible feeling for a while after and I have had to make myself sick once or twice just to get rid of the horrid feeling. Not pleasant at all and in the beginning it was pretty scary.

Even after all of my research until you actually go through something you can never truly know its connotations.

That first Christmas was nowhere near as hard as I had anticipated, foodwise. I had already had a glass of wine early in December and was absolutely fine. I had tried most different food groups and the main things I struggle to tolerate was bread and pasta, both of which gave me the 'foamies.'

I did miss bread, in particular. I would very often have a sandwich for lunch before. Now I had to get a bit more inventive. I would have small meals often, rather than three large meals a day, as recommended with WLS. I sampled small amounts of chocolate and was fine. When I say a small amount, I really do mean small. Two squares and I was completely satisfied. I had been able to enjoy crisps again. I couldn't manage a whole packet and was able to control the desperate need for them that I'd had in the past.

On Christmas day I enjoyed all the foods that I always had during the festive period. Cheeses, chocolate, the main event: the almighty roast, just a taste of an aged pudding with cream and even a small glass of creamy Irish whisky.

I didn't and haven't felt like I was missing out since that first time. In fact, I very quickly got used to my portion sizes and only now and again do I remember what my old plates of food looked like size-wise, and I cringe. I know I am very lucky being able to tolerate these foods. Many people that have bariatric surgery have a very different story to tell and are unable to tolerate anything too sweet or high in fats. It's a bit of a double edge sword really, as I could easily slip into old habits. I know only too well how quickly things can become normalised in your own mind and escalate.

Although the weight is coming off quickly, it's a very gradual change physically. When you say, "Oh I've lost over three stones," you'd expect to see a huge change in appearance, however that wasn't the case for me. Sure, my dress size had reduced but I could still wear the same clothes that I had pre-surgery without them falling off. They were definitely looser, and some were very obviously too big, but I didn't have to go out and replace the whole lot.

Bypassing Obesity

By the time the new year came around, I was able to finally go into a supermarket and get clothes. I was a size twenty-two. At this time we were, once again back in lockdown and so we did what everybody else was doing and purchased an inflatable hot tub. I got a new swimming costume from TU at Sainsburys in a twenty-four and almost cried with joy at being able to wear it.

After another few weeks and another stone down, things dramatically changed, and I was now in need of some new threads. There are not many things that thrill me more than clothes. I didn't have the money to go out and blow vast amounts on a new wardrobe, so I hit the charity shops.

A huge downside of losing weight, for me was losing my beloved items of clothing. I never had a massive amount of clothes but what I did have, I loved. Going through them and having a trying-on session was thrilling yet sad, as some of my most beloved and treasured key pieces were now surplus to requirement and so I ended up selling them to enable me to replace them.

I purchased my first ever top from Next in a size twenty-two, a cute blouse in bottle green with little bees on. That was such a special achievement. Every few days I tried on my special tartan trousers and to my utter shock towards the end of January the bloody things pulled right up and fucking DID UP!! This was probably one of the best feels thus far. I can only *try* to describe the feeling with words, as I don't think there are enough words in the English language to describe it. The mixture of achievement, pride and revelation was not something I was used to. Shock, excitement and a new feeling that took me by surprise as I'd never thought of it before; that of normality. I was no longer one of the biggest in society. I was still obese, around seventeen stone something in weight, but I wasn't the biggest when I went out into the community.

The feeling was somewhat of a revelation to me as I had not ever consciously thought of myself in that way. Sure I knew I was the biggest person in most rooms, but I hadn't ever realised that it bothered me at such an intense level and so a feeling of realisation, relief, and reassurance swept over me all in one hit. I'm not ashamed to say I cried again at the feeling that wearing these trouser gave me.

I mourned deeply for Sarah before and wished I could have told her how special this felt. I felt like I was mourning her for having to live with the burden she had. I felt so very sorry for the 'me' that 'she' had been almost four months ago, because she had no true idea of how desperately unhappy she was.

SEVENTEEN

Gaining so much through loss

You hear quotes about gaining through loss and it often has a connotation of death, deprivation, or dissolution somehow. I guess in some ways the loss of oneself in any term is all of the above, even if the loss is wanted, needed. Just for a moment I am claiming the quote and using it for a positive, desirable attribute. Having to let go of something cannot always be simply a bad thing. After all, by letting go we often become lighter, emotionally-speaking. A silly little thing was letting go of my clothes that had served me so well. However, it made room for a new, smaller sized, broader choice of garments.

Another stone off put me into the sixteen something stone range on the scale. I was cooking on gas now and the loss was bringing me daily gifts that were changing my life so dramatically, it was like living in a movie scene. The gifts stated coming in thick and fast at the eighteen-week post-surgery mark, and at that time I had lost just a fraction over five stones in weight, 71lbs! Those early benefits were astounding and completely life changing as well as life affirming for me. Small things that I never even realised that were problems are now evaporating as the sunshine gleamed into my very soul and cleared the mist I didn't even know was lingering.

Sarah-Jane Oakenfull

One afternoon, my youngest daughter came to give me a hug. I will tell you at this stage she has autism and is very blunt, but also is a sensory seeker who requires deep, firm hugs. She came to me whilst I was standing in front of the fireplace in our lounge. I remember what we were wearing, what I was cooking, and her exact words, because the split second is deeply entwined within my spirit, one of the best moments of my life, ever.

She came in for a hug. I was wearing a navy-blue cotton jumper that I'd got in the charity shop, with jeggings, both a size twenty. She was in her school uniform and the time was 5:35. I was cooking a chicken pie with mash and runner beans.

She put her nine-year-old arms around me and in an almost frightened, it was so high pitched, excited voice she said these beautiful words... "Mummy, I can get my arms around you now you're not too fat".

That second, right there, the earth stopped spinning and the clocks stopped. The world didn't matter, all that was significant at that exact moment in time was this.

This was why I walked into that hospital alone.

This was why I didn't eat solid food for a month, didn't sit at the table for a family meal for a month, why I wanted to shed the heavy burden of obesity, and this is why I wanted to be the healthiest version of myself.

Here I am again, crying, weeping all the emotional gladness like raindrops during a storm, watering the rainbow to help it thrive. It would be nice for me to lose weight if I was alone. But losing it with my family was as fulfilling and rewarding as that rainbow full of colour. No more floods, no more drowning. A promise to myself and to my girls.

Bypassing Obesity

Another evening I sat watching TV, I believe it was a Thursday and the program in question was most probably Coronation Street. I had a sudden realisation that I was sitting with my legs crossed. Not much to the average human being but as I sat watching Steve McDonald in whatever predicament he was in this week, the fact I had my legs crossed was absolutely incredible. You see I had not been able to sit all lady like with my legs crossed for my whole adult life. I do recall sitting cross legged in my youth but as a fully-fledged grown up I had never been able to physically do so. Something so simple that every day people take for granted meant the world to me and it was a huge deal. I pointed my foot out, toes straight like a ballerina, with my left leg draped over my right and did a one eighty with it. I felt very sophisticated and ladylike. It still makes me smile today that I can sit like that you know, it's something I will never take for granted. It's the smallest thing that meant the most, the gaining everything whilst losing.

As stated in earlier chapters, I am somewhat of a loud, showy off character, sorry-not-sorry. So I do take the odd-few selfies. Okay, so I take quite a lot of selfies. One day I was smiling and trying to get a decent enough picture to do a 'before and now' side by side for my WLS blog. I noticed two small holes on each cheek (face). I had dimples. I have dimples. Again, who knew that the round face even on the happiest smiley days had these dimples? Another revelation to me. I felt like I was getting to know myself every single day. Still I felt like I was mourning the 'me' from before, but I feel like she is still locked in and my biggest supporter. Go us!

Lots and lots of firsts followed the hugging day, the arms around me day.

For instance, I always had very fat, swollen feet when I was twenty plus stone. I love clothes and fashion but have always had an issue with shoes. My feet were my arch-nemesis. The summer was sandals with a buckle and the winter was one pair of boots from a special wide fitting range and nothing much in-between. However, currently they had started to appear a more reasonable size, particularly within the first six months. I was able to get some wellington boots for the first time in my adult life. I got bright yellow ones with bumble bees adorned. The muddy dog walks were changed for me the day I could wear them, and I had no excuses to stay home in wet weather.

Whilst talking feet, I also managed to get myself a pair of Converse. This was a really, really big deal to me. I had always wanted a pair, but I could never get them on my huge, poor feet. When I slipped the white pair on and did them up, I was choked up. What a day that was. From then on, I wore them at every opportunity and always pointed them out to family and friends. It was such a proud feeling for me.

The pride I felt in myself had been so unusual to begin with, but as the months rolled on, I was finding it easier to accept and own these newfound feelings.

Okay, the next thing that stands out as a particularly significant moment is a fashion related one. Jumpsuits. I have always loved jumpsuits. I have also always, in my adult years, had a very large, hanging tummy. The two do not, on me, bode well. I have seen plenty of large ladies looking absolutely fabulous in an all-in-one, however I look fucking hideous! My tummy just hung too low and was just too big. I just didn't feel comfortable nor confident in one. So the day my new burnt-orange jumpsuit arrived, I was itching to try it on but must admit I did have an intrepid feeling too, after all this was completely uncharted territory for me. A true size twenty at this stage, I went upstairs to my bedroom and pulled on the soft, jersey number. Oh my god, it fit and even better than that, it looked sensational. I was on cloud nine. No tears today but lots of Cheshire Cat grinning.

Bypassing Obesity

In the April, we had a family weekend booked. Two of my brothers and their families, both of my sisters and my dad and step mum, myself and my family all packed up and drove to Yorkshire for a belated, due to Covid, mini-break.

It had been a Christmas present from the parents, the year that COVID-19 rocked the world. Now we finally had the greenlight from the government to go ahead and meet up. It takes around five hours to drive to the Dales and the first difference to me whilst on the long journey was how comfortable I was in the seat of the car, and also I didn't have to stop every hour for a wee.

I hadn't had the opportunity to see my dad for a long while, so I was really excited to see him and reveal myself. I had lost around seven stone at this point, so it had made a huge dent in my appearance. Of course I had sent photos but the look on my dad's face when he set eyes on me that day was so special. I felt like we made a great team, my dad provided me with the funds to change my life. He gave me a tool to use and I had hammered the shit out of it, which is very apt as my dad is a successful builder.

We had an amazing few days, the weather was incredible and all the children behaved themselves, that was a first for all of us. Another particular first for me that weekend was sitting next to my eldest daughter in a playground, on a swing. It was the first ever time I had fit into a swing, and it was joyful to sit side by side and have childish fun with my almost teenage daughter. We giggled and swung so high I thought I might fly away, the emotional feeling of sharing this with my first born was just as wonderful as the physical feeling. That weekend we walked, and I kept up, we ate and drank, and I never once felt left out or deprived. We had a wonderful weekend.

The stall, an inevitable irritant

It happened. The stall.

The weight loss stalled. This is an inevitable part of the process. I have had so many messages from people asking whether I had had any stalls during my weight loss. The thing is, after losing such a lot of weight at such a rapid rate, when the stall comes, it's almost a disappointing shock. It's a concern when, in the midst of your loss, going strong, the weight is coming off, and them *BAM*, nothing.

When you have such a vast amount to lose and are, roughly halfway through it's absolutely gutting to stall. You get very used to very quickly losing so much weight, especially as your body is changing and people are noticing the changes, that when it stops, all be it temporarily, you feel a bit of a letdown and wonder what on earth you are doing wrong.

My stall was for almost a month. It was the beginning of the summer and I was comfortably wearing a size twenty still. I really wanted to push to get into an eighteen but the scales nor the number in my clothes where moving. I wasn't cheating, I couldn't. I was exercising as much as I could. I had even started doing a keep fit class via YouTube every morning at home. I'm not one for the gym, it's just not for me.

I had lost around eight stone at this stage, and I could now fit in to my mum's clothes which was amazing. I had been given Next vouchers for my birthday and had treated myself to a new dress. As extremely marvellous and self-inspiring that was, the stall made me feel a bit low again for a hot minute. Always a contradiction, I also felt bloody brilliant and can honestly say if I had stayed at that size I would have been proud of myself and confident as ever. After being so very big that everyday tasks were a graft, being that much smaller was mind blowing. I was able to move easier and felt less constricted. I felt much more energised and was able to walk longer, get upstairs without feeling like I had run a marathon and, on a few occasions, chased the girls upstairs for being rude. They were both surprised and annoyed at that.

Bypassing Obesity

For three weeks I weighed myself with no movement. I re-checked my diet but in reality there was nothing I could do any differently to re-kick start. I'll say again in a counterstatement that I was feeling content with my size. I felt like I fit into society now. People had stopped staring at me so much, men had started to open doors for me and smile. I felt less judged if I am completely honest. I felt like people had stopping looking and wondering what on earth I ate or how I managed to operate at such a size. I guess I was more 'normal' now.

Many people I have spoken with really struggle with the stall. They feel like they are failing themselves. You know that in general if you undergo the mammoth ordeal of bariatric surgery that you are going to lose a lot of weight, so when that slows down or stops before you're ready, it can feel very confusing and frustrating. So many people get really upset and that's completely understandable. However it isn't always a permanent thing. Stay calm and carry on! There is always hope, even in the most challenging times.

Personally, I had to keep looking back at how far I had come and remind myself of exactly what a bloody superstar I am. Dory, just keep swimming, even though it's upstream and it feels like you're not getting very anywhere. Eventually the tide turns and even if that means learning to live with where you are right now and accept that this is the new you, the chances are it is just a stall, a temporary bump the weight-loss road.

The stall makes you question your dietary needs and every tiny thing that passes your lips is examined and scrutinised. The whole ethos of food after weight-loss surgery is protein. Protein is key and the building block of the WLS menus. The first thing that has to cross your mind when choosing your meals is, how much protein has it got? Our body needs it to survive and thrive, along with the balance to fresh fruit and vegetables, fats, sugars and carbs in small quantities, but the biggest change diet-wise is protein is the alpha and the omega, the buck stops with the big P.

I found it really hard the first few months, even after all the research. I even stared to eat more protein before my operation in preparation. I really quickly got sick of chicken. Eggs were another thing that became a chore to eat. Nowadays I eat a lot of beans and pulses. A bean chilli is my go-to meal for a hit if I'm seeking something away from meat. For about two months I would have a Dairylea Dunker for lunch and a Babybel cheese.

The stall is an inevitable part of weight-loss surgery. There are those exceptions of the rule, of course. The lucky ones who sail through the processes like a well-worn yachtsman. For those of us that get hit by the stall, we have to remember just what a huge ordeal our bodies have been through. Really, it is a traumatic thing for our bodies to go though, particularly a body that has already been carrying obesity. It takes time and a certain amount of adjustment for the body to processes the rapid changes.

At first it's almost like a tap of weight just flooding out but sooner or later the tap must ease. The body needs to find its metabolic balance. This isn't just part of bariatric surgery but weight-loss in general. Now and then our anatomy needs to stop and re group, readjust and then start again.

Life after weight loss surgery is just that, a life after. As long as I am taking my vitamins and keeping up with my B12 injections, I eat a good amount of protein and am exercising as much as I can, then the stalls are just stalls and not a permanent state. Even if I had lost just a stone and then stalled, it would have been a stone less for my knees and feet to carry.

EIGHTEEN

The livin is easy, summertime

The slow trumpets at the start, the easy rhythm and lazy melody literally sings to me. Then all of a sudden Ella Fitzgerald smacks you in the face with her tone. *Summertime and the living is easy*.

Shut your eyes and picture what an easy summer looks like. Slow but steady, almost fluid like alongside the heat of the long stretching days. Summer is here and the living is easy, it's all so different. It feels like the first ever summer of my life and all of a sudden I notice that the fish are swimming and the birds are flying high. I notice the beauty and ease of summer and not just a heat that delivers limitations and restrictions.

As an obese woman, summer has always been a foe. The reality of living with chub rub was amplified greatly during the summer months and was extremely painful as, even with cycling shorts on, the seams seemed to rub and there were days and weeks of discomfort from the chaffing. The heat affected my already swollen feet and they ballooned uncomfortably every year and looked almost as if they had been stuck on the end of my legs. They were tight and very uncomfortable; I had a real concern that they would one day seep with whatever fluid had flooded them. Under my breast and tummy would be sore and angry at me. I wore a bra with a flannel under each breast to stop the rubbing and capture some of the moisture that the heat made me extrude in excess.

Summer made my mind and soul happy and free. I love the colours it brings, the feel of the heat on your skin and the smells of school holidays, barbecues, chlorine and scented blooms, sun cream and freshly cut grass.

Summer made my body very difficult to live in. Being so heavy is a task in itself. To move the body that carries morbid obesity takes effort and hard graft at times. Although the gain is slow and the body adjusts to carrying the weight at that pace, it seems to all of a sudden scream at you, "I can't do this!" Even the strain of the simplest tasks is heightened, add hot repressive weather to the mix and the tasks become almost impossible.

A physical tiredness came over me in the summer months as my body tried to stay cool and function under the stresses of obesity and heat combination. Walking ten minutes felt like an hour and even the school run, a chore, became my daily exercise, my only exercise.

Although we were outside a lot, mainly at the beach, when I was sat down, that was me. Unless I needed the toilet I barely moved. I would try and make sandcastles if the kids were next to me and I'd always try to get up and go looking under rocks for crabs and such like. Sat on my big old bottom it was like I was fixed to the spot, sweating profusely and convincing myself that I would rather watch the family out on the calm, reflective water, paddle boarding than I would join in.

Bypassing Obesity

As I approached the first summer, I had lost eight stone. I was between a size eighteen and sixteen. I always had a secret goal way back in the recess of my mind that a size sixteen was the ultimate. I was almost there. That summer hosted a string of firsts for me and every single day I had an almost-epiphany at what life was like in the summer for someone without carrying obesity.

We went on a family day out to a little place in Norfolk. It's a woodland adventure, with big wooden structures and slides, zip-wires and a little boat trip. I was wearing my Converse; still unbelievable how happy it can make you just to have a pair of shoes that you have longed for and for the shoes to not only fit but be incredibly comfortable too.

I was really excited for this day as it was not only the first fun day after lock-down but since losing weight too. The day started with a bit of trepidation. I have always been the bag holder on days out. I'd find a place to sit and watch the family enjoying themselves and I would stay there and look over the bags and picnic.

Always an outsider, I had buried the feelings of longing and desperation so deep that an envious glow would often overcome me whilst I watch the family, laughing, living and enjoying. I used to watch other families and resent them deeply, the mums full of energy and able to join in, to have the choice in whether or not to participate. Those mums seemed to be the ultimate parents. They would climb up onto park climbing frames and sit on swings next to their children, they were doing it properly, being involved in the day, being involved in life.

Sometimes I would catch myself watching families with disabled parents that could participate but were not able-bodied enough to do certain tasks. An enormous weight of guilt would make me perspire. I had, after all, brought this on myself, however subconsciously. Some people have no choice but still manage to be involved and thrive whilst doing so.

Sarah-Jane Oakenfull

Now and again the amour of humour and self-shaming would slip, and the bubbly fat girl would melt away. The true burden would emerge, and I lost my fake smile and retreat into a guilt-ridden shame. Now I just looked the miserable fat woman, too fat to join in. I felt that when I let the mask slip people were even more judgmental towards me. Look at the unhappy obese woman, why doesn't she just stop eating? Why indeed.

Not today. Today was my first ever inclusive day out with my family. Okay so the girls were arguing and had been all sodding night in the hotel we had stayed in. My husband and I had to separate them and sleep in one of the two double beds with one child each. We were all tired and just a bit grumpy, that didn't piss on my parade.

When we arrived, I subconsciously took in the pathways and noted the amount of walking this was going to involve. Then I remembered that it was within my realms of capability. Tiredness evaporated and something like excitement came over me, I skipped. Not many mums were skipping, just me, a forty-year-old, still overweight, mum of two, skipping like a five-year-old child.

We walked for a bit, taking in the beauty of the woods and all the small characters hidden in amongst the trees and bracken, following the trails. We came to the first set of wooden climbing structures, armed with a zip wire and narrow rope bridges, tunnels and small alcoves. I climbed the wooden ladder up to the first platform that had another ladder up to the second one that housed the rope bridge. I must have looked like a psychopath because I was giggling like a bloody crazed in-patient, on the verge of tears, filled with nothing but joy.

This was living.

I was joining in. I zipwired and climbed. I went on the deathslide and I kept up with the kids. On a few of the slides, my husband had to sit with the bags so that I could have a go, and another go. I didn't care about having to walk far, or climb up some steps, I just did it.

Bypassing Obesity

They had a little boat trip around a small lake and down into a stream. It had all the little fairy characters along the way and a few surprises for the kids. I got on the boat and floated along like everyone else. No smart remarks or jokes about my weight to reflect and avoid humiliation by others. I just got on the damn boat and enjoyed it.
It was like being born again.

The day was an eye-opener. A revelation and a huge success. Now don't get me wrong, the girls nit-picked at each other all day and my husband moaned about the price of the coffee, how much an ice-cream was and did they really deserve one anyway. It was an average day out, expensive and not without its ructions, but for me it was like day one, the first of many more physically able firsts.

Just to name a few, here are some of the following firsts: Roller skating. I didn't fall over but only because I didn't really move that fast. I clung to the rail and moved an inch at a time around the enormous rink. Terrified that I would fall and break my arm, or neck.

I took part in, should I say, participated in a mud race with my girls and their cousins. It involved very deep trench of thick oozy mud with rope swings above, lots of walking, lots of sliding around like a buffoon during a monsoon. Think of those sexy, mud wrestling games that the youngsters liked in the late nineties and then imagine the absolute polar opposite. I wasn't very good and to be completely honest. I hated being wet, cold and muddy. But I still bloody did it.

That summer consisted of zipwiring at every given opportunity, swinging myself high into the air at every park we visited. That summer had boat trips in Norfolk to see seals. It had me climbing up on to huge, square, haybales in the farmer's field behind our house, after harvest, in a magical, cerise-pink sunset, dancing like a drunk dad at a disco. It was simply liberating.

NINETEEN

Moroccan sunset

I mentioned that shortly before my weight loss surgery my dear old Grandpa Music sadly died. I have also forementioned that my Mum has always struggled financially, maybe starting my food related issues due to not having much in the way of treats.

Well, my grandpa had left mum an inheritance and a fairly substantial one too. Mum, for the first time ever was able to treat herself to almost anything she wanted and was able to have a brand-new bed with mattress for the first time. She got herself new bedroom furniture and booked a holiday. It was so great to see mum treating herself. If she saw a top she liked, she simply brought it. Liked a pair of shoes, she got them!

We sat in her lounge one afternoon and joked about having a little holiday, just the two of us. At this point although I had lost a huge amount of weight, around nine stone, life was a bit of a slog. Having a children can be a difficult and thankless task but having a child with additional needs can be another level of shite all together. No amount of weight-loss can cure the fatigue that parenting presents to you. Sure it does really help but life within any family is, at times gruelling.

Sarah-Jane Oakenfull

With the school holidays coming to a close, I was feeling fragile and tearful. The last six weeks had been brilliant, physically but emotionally I was exhausted. Mum and I laughed and started looking at mini breaks on our phones and I came across a three-night break to Marrakesh. It was under £300 for an adults-only (selling point) all-inclusive, five-star resort. It was for a date in September, just eighteen days away.

We only went and fucking booked it!

I called my husband and asked him if it was okay for him to take some time off work and have the girls, do the school run, etcetera. Thank God he said yes because we had already booked the holiday.

My mum and I were off on a Shirley Valentine trip (minus the fling), and we suddenly got a bit nervous. We hadn't been on holiday together on our own for forty years, when I was two and we visited Grandpa and Nanny in Canada whilst they lived there for a short time.

I had no swimming costume that fit and with it being the end of summer, we had only the dregs of sun-cream. With the weight-loss still falling swiftly after my stall, I had minimal clothes worthy of a holiday. So, I hit the chazza (charity shop) hard. My love of charity shops started at a young age. With mum being so hard up we would always look in the chazzas before anywhere else. In those days it wasn't fashionable to dress in second hand clothes, but I always loved it. I loved wondering about the back story of an item, who had worn it and what had it seen prior to me? I loved the smell too. Many hate the smell of a chazza, but I have always loved it, that and the smell of hospitals.

My local chazza is a huge warehouse that has all the items that didn't sell at the High Street charity shops. It is vast and extremely exciting. I managed to find some dresses and a pantsuit, as well as some swimwear too. I was made up. I had my chazza haul and most of the clothes where a size……. SIXTEEN!!! unbelievable. I was gobsmacked. Astounded. I treated myself to a… bikini! Who even am I?

Bypassing Obesity

All packed and ready to go, Mum and I started to behave a little bit strangely. It was as if a childlike hue had adorned us. By the time we got to the airport, late I might add, we barely made it in time, we were acting like silly teenagers, just giggling and smirking at each other.

We found a bar and sat with a drink and some lunch and awaited our flight number to be displayed on screen so we could head to the correct gate. At the gate we waited patiently to board the plane, still smiling like dick heads. It felt so easy, and I hadn't felt so free in a long time. It had been years since mum or I had flown anywhere, what with the worldwide pandemic and with being poor and all that. It's funny at airports, all manner of people to watch and wonder who they are, where they are going and why. Busy-people-watching in an easy silence you can only have with your very nearest and dearest and then with the odd few conversations scattered, the announcement was made, we were to board our flight to Morocco.

Not quite believing we were actually doing this, we headed down the tube towards the aircraft. It's almost like going into bloody space, the metal tunnel connecting the port to the craft.

Once on board we made our way towards our seats, I was struck at how wide the aisles were. Then struck again at the fact they were not any wider, I was smaller. I fit. I didn't have to crabwalk sideways down the aisles like the shellfish walk of shame. No-one stared at me. I was invisible. I was 'normal'.

Mum and I weren't seated together, due to being so sodding late. However we were seated next to each other, with the aisle separating us. Mum sat with a couple off on their holidays, and I had the whole row of three seats to myself, happy days. Mum got settled in her seat whilst I put our hand luggage away in the overhead compartments. I got my phone and headphones out, ready for the journey. I had downloaded some music just for the trip, something new and different. Alabama Shakes, upbeat and soulful, perfect. I had also downloaded my dear Miriam's autobiography, as read by herself, in her own tongue. I was so excited and free, it was an incredible feeling.

Sarah-Jane Oakenfull

Then I sat down.

Then I put on my seat belt.

I put on my seat belt.

I actually sat on an aeroplane and put on a seatbelt. No calling the steward for an extender, no humorous jokes, I just sat and did it. With the background song, 'Hold On' in my ears as sung by Alabama Shakes, I'd done it. I had held on and here I was, an average person, on a plane, going on a trip with my mum.

I felt like I was living in a movie to be honest. I'm just a regular woman, who had lost nearly ten stone, with two daughters and a husband, autism was impacting life everyday (some positively, some not so much). I had survived the kids' summer holidays and now I was jetting off. I even had my own soundtrack. I cried again, through a massive smile, looking out of an air-plane window, with mum next to me (aisle aside). I felt so fucking empowered, right there, right then.

The hotel was just beautiful, so relaxed and, because there were no children, it just felt ridiculously zen. After the flight and baggage collection, the short coach trip, and the hot humid air in our lungs we sat outside on a rattan sofa. We had our first taste of a Moroccan meal. We just stared at each other and grinned like kids again, we actually couldn't believe we were there. We raised a glass to Grandpa before the end of day, ready for our first full day in the Moroccan sun. Oh, did I mention that our room had a jacuzzi on the balcony?
The entire holiday was wonderful. The sun was hot, and the food was delicious, the drinks were plenty, and the company was perfect. Mum and I got on so well and Morocco was amazing.

Bypassing Obesity

The way I felt on that holiday was something new, it was a chance for me to re-find my new self. Such a corny cheese fest but it's true. I'm still the same person as I was before weight-loss, but we are supposed to change and evolve, re-evaluate our lives and that's what I did in those few days.

I walked in the souks, taking in every smell and sight I could, I felt soft leather and smiled at strangers, I ate spices I'd never tried before. I started to live, not only physically. I found Sarah, the old, new Sarah. I was able to walk in a dress with no shorts on. I had no chub rub. It was thirty-six degrees and I walked without chub rub.

One evening mum was feeling really tired and after a lot of walking she was aching and needed to rest. I got dressed up and went down and had dinner alone. I felt great. I got myself a glass of wine and sat in a quiet spot and just enjoyed every second of the heat in my lungs and the peace in my ears. I felt so empowered by booking and jetting off on this mini break. Not as mum, not as wife or friend, not as a fat person but just as me. A strong woman.

Mum and I enjoyed an evening on a rooftop in Morocco with a glass of champagne, watching the sunset over the maze of souks Marrakesh possessed and I think that's where I realised that I didn't need to be jolly, attention-seeking Sarah anymore. I could just be myself and not have to make people try to like me, to see through my size. I no longer needed assurance.

I had profound contentment.

TWENTY

Defying gravity

Something has changed within me; something is not the same.

Some days in our lives we feel as if we are walking on air. Some days we feel like we have crash landed on to planet earth and the weight of the world is upon us. Life after weight loss is no exception. Yes, there are so many great things that living without obesity is made much, much better for. There is not much or at least nothing I can think of that is worse for not being obese. However, losing weight is not an aid for having bad days. It does not cure depression, anxiety or low mood. Addiction is still an issue whatever size you are.

Most of the time these days, I do feel as if I am defying gravity and I look to the western skies like the witch in *Wicked*. I can only speak for myself and my own experience and that has been amazing for me, but I do know of people that have had weight loss surgery and regretted it deeply. It's not for everyone.

There are lifetime sacrifices after having the operation, that sometimes can be difficult to live with. Just small, silly things like not being able to eat and drink at the same time or not being able to have a fizzy drink is sometimes a drag.

Personally, the sacrifice is worth it and if I feel down about the little things, it's only a fleeting thought. The benefits far, far outweigh any negatives for me. At times I crave a huge meal. I want to stuff my face and mop up the gravy on my plate with a greasy Yorkshire pudding. I can't do that. Now and again for a second or two, I wish I could. Then I remember my daughter's arms wrapped right around me.

Whilst walking on air and feeling like you are defying gravity is wonderful, I always have the old Sarah in the back of my mind. I remember how it felt to see someone you knew or perhaps even didn't know, losing weight. When you are in the clutches of obesity and the future seems to be creeping up on you with no plausible route out, you feel very trapped, then you eat more. I always felt very happy for losers-in-weight, but it is only natural to feel envy too. I wish I could do that; I wish it was me.

I feel ashamed to say that I have felt bitter in the past, seeing people escape obesity, thinking that my time would never come. I felt like I deserved to stay this way, I had done this to myself, yet I could not control it. I was so very envious. In my thirties I always said I would rather be fat than have to live with the excess skin that weight-loss would cause. I held on to that, my armour, until I almost believed it myself. My Facebook profile was spammed with post and quotes about big, beautiful women and I do still believe that you can be big and absolutely stunning, just look at Alison Hammond for goodness's sake.

I didn't believe it of myself or for myself. When I look back, I was putting up a wall to protect myself from admitting that living my life as a morbidly obese person was affecting my ability to function day-to-day in the simplest of activities. I think when I came out and told my little part of the social media world what I was doing, people might have been surprised, the one that was spreading the word about being confident in your own skin wasn't actually confident at all.

My reason for this explanation is to say that, as I was losing weight and the contentment set in, I started to feel a confidence in myself and my own abilities.

Bypassing Obesity

I was finding day-to-day life really easy now and all the things I had struggled to do before were now just drops in the ocean. I wanted to shout that from the rooftops. I wanted the world to know that there is another life, one that is full of ease and comfort.

I looked back at myself, and I felt a huge sadness. The old Sarah, the morbidly obese, twenty-three stone plus woman would have been hurt if she had heard someone saying such things and it made me think that possibly other obese people would also feel hurt. Some of those are my friends. I started to feel guilty towards myself from two years ago.

I honestly had no idea that I would feel this way once I had lost weight, I just thought I would be healthier and more able-bodied. The realisation that the confident front I had put on made me so very sad and the fact that I was floating on air made me feel even sadder. It sounds a bit strange to be referring to myself as a third person, in past tense but that's the only way I can describe it.

It was coming up to a year since my weight loss surgery and I was getting all melancholic about it. With such a massive life event and the changes it had given me, the life it had presented to me, it seemed like a good time to get out some of my old clothes that I had kept. A pair of jeans and a shirt, the jeans where a size thirty and the shirt a thirty-two. I could now fit myself into one leg of the jeans. Instead to feeling elated, I felt so sad for my previous self. If only I had known what life could have been like without obesity, would I have tried harder? Had I let myself down?

The answer is no.

I didn't consciously chose obesity, it chose me, and it gripped me like a constrictor squeezing its prey.

I cried when I tried on those jeans, it made me feel so sad. There is an epidemic in this country, and it needs to be addressed. It's not as contagious as Covid, or as widely caught as the common cold, but it is here, and it kills people.

Sarah-Jane Oakenfull

Obesity is an epidemic and there are human beings out there suffering, living it every single day, and I don't think many, if any, of those actively sought out obesity or consciously chose it. Without getting into politics, there has to be help, understanding and education on obesity. As a survivor of the fucking thing, I can now see what life can be like without it and I truly think everyone should be important enough to feel what life is like when you defy gravity.

The surgery-versary day came and I got the train up to visit my dad and step mum to take them out for lunch, a birthday treat if you will. Well I missed my train, running late again (theme), and had to purchase a second ticket so I was out of pocket. I ended up getting us fish and chips, but we had a good time and I think they were pleased that I had made an effort to travel up and show them just how grateful and humble I am to them for giving me the opportunity to kick obesity's arse. It had been one whole year, and I was just over ten stone lighter.

The year came to a close and I had picked myself up and realised that although I will always feel a sadness towards my old self, I have to live and thrive right now. I have a lot more to experience without the burden. I also have to tell people what being obese feels like, to spread awareness and ultimately shout from the rooftops, "We did not consciously choose to be obese. It was not ever my childhood ambition."

I had a lot to look forward to in the coming year. Day to day life was immeasurably easier. The school run, shopping and walking the dog was no longer a 'thing' it was just a daily task, bit like brushing your teeth. It no longer involved a huge amount of effort and small things like getting upstairs no longer left me panting and out of breath.

Suddenly I found that I no longer made excuses not to pop upstairs if I'd forgotten something. If I was going to a friend's whose bathroom was upstairs, I no longer waited until I was desperate, or dreaded having to heave myself up there.

Bypassing Obesity

Other toilet related issues had evaporated too. I could now hold my bladder. Sounds silly but when I was twenty-three stone, I literally needed a wee all the bloody time and couldn't hold it for toffee. Within the family I was always being taken the 'piss' out of because I always needed a wee. Now I could hold a wee for an impressive amount of time. Impressive to me was longer than ten minutes. I didn't start holding my bladder for hours and hours, that might end in a disaster.

It's a really liberating thing to not be held back by your bladder and the number of stairs that lead you to the required facilities. Journeys were so much more enjoyable now that we didn't have to stop every half hour for me to waddle into services and relieve myself then waddle back out.

That year did provide me some journeys too. I had a trip up to Yorkshire with my cousin to visit dearest Nana. We drove up and stayed in a hotel for a few nights. Two mums having a little break whilst spending time with our Nana was really great. We went for some walks around the Dales, and I didn't once feel like I was slowing my cousin down. My nana has also lived with obesity and so when she saw me now after losing nearly eleven stone, she was beside herself. I had made her very proud, and she was incredibly supportive.

We managed to take her out on a picnic to Bolton Abby. We took a whole tea service complete with cake stand, cups and saucers, tea pot and milk jug. We laid on a seafood platter and scones with clotted cream and had a truly fabulous day. That was a day I'll remember forever.

Before my surgery I went to meet up with a lady I knew through Facebook, and through my sister-in-law. She had had a sleeve and then went on to have a bypass. She had lost a lot of weight and was full of encouragement. She told me to hold on to my hat, it was gonna be a bumpy trip. She wasn't wrong.

I had been able to meet up with a friend of a friend, not long after my surgery. Goldie had had her surgery though the NHS tiers and was having huge success. She was really open and honest with me about what to expect in the coming months. She even gave me some clothes which I absolutely loved.

The thing about being obese and then going through WLS is that it can feel very isolating and lonely. To meet up with someone who had been through it and understood every query and question was such a help.

Another event that happened that year was through my blog. I has posted a picture of myself outside the private hospital that I had my weight loss surgery at. A lady had got in touch with me saying that she was due to go and meet with the surgeon 'Mr J' for her first appointment regarding WLS. Her name was Emma and we started to message each other, then eventually we met up with some others that had had the same surgeon at the same hospital.

One thing struck me at this point, all of us were normal, everyday people, not rich, all hard working. All of us had the weight loss surgery paid for by our families in one way or another. Not one of us had the funds to simply go off and get £10,000 worth of private medical care on a whim. I find this really interesting. Some of us had been turned down by the NHS and some had simply gone straight down the private route. One thing we all agreed on was that it was worth every inch of pain, every penny spent and every bad moment we had had on the way.

I just wonder out of the six of us who would still be obese forever if we had not had bariatric surgery and what that might have cost the NHS in the long run.
Emma and I hit it off the first second we met and had a really comfortable, easy friendship. It didn't feel like the first time we had met; it really was like we had known each other for years. We had the same views on lots of subjects and although Emma is younger than me, we had the same sense of humour too. So when she asked me if I wanted to go to an event, she had seen advertised I jumped at the chance.

Bypassing Obesity

'The Bariatric Ball' was an event for obese people and survivors, that had had or are considering having weight-loss surgery. An inclusive, non-judgmental occasion for likeminded individuals of all ages, stages, genders and sizes to get together and dance, let go and enjoy being amongst others who have or are living with obesity.

Remember that weight-loss surgery is not a cure for obesity. It is a tool, and a successful one in most cases, but not the only option to aid in the fight against obesity. It is an expensive, long road and is a drastic decision to make. If the NHS deem you legible for the surgery it is a bloody long road, years in-fact. You have to undergo years of therapy and tests of strength to be considered for it. It is an individual process and not any one person's is the same as another.

What I found interesting was meeting people that had had enormous success and gone on to have the skin removal surgery too. Some of the younger women looked like models, absolutely stunning.

As I sat and looked around the room, I was struck at how many people where there, but also the 'types' of people. I couldn't have imagined that some of these people had ever been fat. Some of the people there had lost fifteen stone or more. One man had lost over twenty stone, that's like two extra human beings and what was very interesting was, he said that he wished he had never had bariatrics surgery. With it being a party with disco and us all dressed in our finery it didn't feel like the time to press him about the whys and what ifs, but I did manage to hear him say that the excess skin was a huge issue for him. I could have wept for this brave man; he had beaten obesity and kicked its arse so fucking hard but had regrets. It was one of the saddest things I had heard in all the individual journeys. It goes to show that it is not for everyone and is as much an emotional journey as a physical one.

Sarah-Jane Oakenfull

That night I felt the most beautiful I had ever felt in my life. I looked in the mirror and thought yeah, I would! I had got myself a new, second hand, long 1920s repo dress that came down in a low V at the front, all sequinned in art deco-style triangles. It had a split up the middle from the front of the dress too and was really sexy. I also got myself a flapper style head piece in diamonds (fake, obviously) from eBay for £5. My entire outfit had cost about £23 including a new, hold-in body suit for underneath the dress.

Emma looked stunning in a navy, lacy dress, her long dark hair all glossy and thick. She was an absolute pro at makeup and looked sensational. We had a brilliant night, we danced, like proper no one's watching danced. We had only met twice but shared a room and it wasn't awkward at all, just really chilled.

It's funny really, the thing we are trying our hardest to escape, obesity, has brought us people together, people like us that might not have ever met. It has built friendships on a foundation of understanding and commonality. A supportive and genuine gladness within a journey of loss.

TWENTY-ONE

Relationships

Every relationship we have with another human being, whether it be as friend or foe is based on our tolerance and commitment.

Time changes every single relationship we have had or will ever have. We, as human beings evolve within our understandings, our experiences change us. Events in our lives change us and that's okay. It's growth and we are meant to bloom and open our minds to changes. Times and situations within our lives change us. Take having children, suddenly you are a parent and your whole reason for living is changed. You are now a protector, a carer and a guardian. Death and grief change our outlook and ultimately our very being, how can it not? Even the smallest situation or event can give us a broader outlook and change our views. Maybe a certain someone from school that you really disliked turns out to be the nurse that helps you through a rough patch, health-wise. Seeing a beautiful sunset or thunderstorm can change our paths just as easily as a huge life event. Change is inevitable and can only be a good thing.

My relationship with my daughters, the most important of all my relationships, has changed with the loss of obesity.

Sarah-Jane Oakenfull

Being an obese parent can be painfully tough. Not being physically able to do some tasks, particularly when the girls were toddlers was the trickiest.

I remember one day when my youngest was about three years old. We were in the park and she was always a climber, a runner and a bit of a menace. She sprinted out of the park towards a road. I tried to run. My huge stomach audibly smacking as I attempted to run after her. Dread seeped through my veins. I couldn't catch her.

Thinking quickly was always my strength with the girls in those days and I suddenly shouted, screamed, "Look! A horse doing a poo!" Luckily, she had no idea that the likeliness of a horse being in the local park on a random, rainy, afternoon in February was slim and she stopped still like a statue. This enabled me to catch up and grab her.

Now she has a diagnosis of autism, and we know why she had/has little-to-no danger awareness. I always had her on reins, her lead as we called it back then. That particular day I had trusted her not to be a flight risk. Rookie error.

When my eldest was small she would always ask me to join her on slides and swings at the park. She is our first born and I had a point to prove about being an obese parent and so I did crafts and arts daily. She had only very balanced meals and no junk. I dressed her beautifully and always had comments from strangers about how 'well kept' she was.

I went to all the baby groups and did a baby massage class with her. Sitting on the floor in a musty church hall was pretty hard at twenty stone. Just getting down on the floor with a newborn, then having to heave myself up with her was a huge effort and although not one person ever commented, you could see that they wondered how I managed. I would often lay her down first so I could set myself down.

Bypassing Obesity

When she started walking it became harder, although she was a very pleasant girl with a soft-hearted soul, and not very often would I have to try and catch her. We had fun times, just Eldest and I. I was a doing-mum, always sat at a table or on the floor with her. However, I always wanted to climb and swing with her, I wanted to be involved. At parties I wanted to bounce on the inflatables with her but physically, I could not.

I have spoken to my daughters today and asked them to tell me if they think our relationships have changed since I have lost weight and what they think the differences are, having a big mum then a smaller mum.

Youngest said that she didn't think I had changed, I was just Mum. Then she said, "Well you can do more things now." She went on to say that she feels like I don't shout so much now and it's good that she can fit into my clothes. Although she also said that most of my clothes are 'weird'. The main thing she likes now is that she can lift me up. She is a strong kid, but she feels really chuffed that she can pick up her mum, get her arms around me for a tight hug and can sit beside me on fairground rides. There is now a lap for her to sit on.

The teenager was a little more forthcoming and profound. The eldest is in full teenage mode and is a bit pissed off that her mum can get into her clothes, a huge embarrassment for her. She was reluctant at first but has told me that although I am still an inconvenient embarrassment to her, I am now less so. She said that she would often have comments from her friends and worry that people would tease her for having such a big mum.

Although my size was incredibly usual to them, as they got older, I would tell them relentlessly that it wasn't healthy or average to be the size I was. The last thing I wanted for them is to be so normalised to obesity that they would themselves become burdened with it also.

Eldest has also said that I do more with them now than I did before. She said I'm still grumpy and moody but the main change in our relationship is that I'm able to do more with the family and she is less embarrassed than she was of me, although apparently I'm still a huge source of shame for her (glad to know I ain't lost my touch).

I also asked the girls if they thought mine and their dad's relationship had changed and, if so, how. They both responded by saying that we argue less now, and when we do, "You argue back to dad more than before." They said that it felt like I can do more stuff, it is better for all four of us as a family. From the mouths of babes.
They have a point, you know, about me arguing back more nowadays. I'll explain why but I know that the Sarah from before would fiercely deny it. The obese version of me would be offended by my analogy of why I fight back more now and stand my ground.

I simply feel more deserving now.

I'm almost ashamed to admit it, but it is the truth. As an obese person, I felt grateful that I had found someone to love me and care for me, want to start a family and build a life with me. I felt almost indebted to my husband for keeping me regardless of my size and so if we had disagreements I always backed down and apologised even when I wasn't in the wrong (most of the time).

This drove my husband bloody mad, I literally burst into tears and said sorry for every and anything. He didn't fall in love with me despite my obesity, nor because of it. He just liked me, my views and my nature.

Bypassing Obesity

I wasn't morbidly obese when we met back at school, I was just fat back then. The morbidity was so gradual that I don't think any of us truly noticed how big I was until now, when we look back at pictures. I felt like I had to appease and adhere to others because I was so grateful to be loved. My husband is not a jealous man in the slightest and I have always assumed that was simply part of having an obese spouse. The assumption that perhaps an obese person is such a niche market, that it would be a very slim (pun) chance for them to meet someone who is attracted to them, therefore unlikely to have the opportunity to be unfaithful. I truly believed that was why my husband never voiced any doubts nor jealous streaks at all. His black and white way of looking at the world had perhaps helped him to see that I was an unlikely target for affection.

In doing research and talking to people that are obese, overweight or have shed stones and beaten the burden of morbid obesity, I have heard many, many times that after successful weight loss, along with changing bodies and confidence, the relationships with their partners can become strained. Suddenly the loser has opened themselves up to a wider market, sexually and attractively speaking. It can leave the other half of the couple feeling suddenly vulnerable and envious. To lose a huge amount of weight brings attention from people that wouldn't necessarily usually communicate with you. People want to know how you've done it, social media and in person. The questions roll off the tongue of the onlookers. Some partners find it too much, after being almost shielded from it before.

Equally, the obese person can often feel as if they have settled. To be loved when you don't love much of yourself is a gift, is it not? This is not true of everyone of course we as obese human beings are individuals, and no two people are the same. I can only speak from what I have learnt and heard from lots of different obese/formally obese people in doing research for other opinions and angles.

The feeling of having settled can be a really awful feeling within a relationship. The love is there but would it have been there if I had not been obese? Would I have not just felt grateful that someone, anyone finds me attractive?

Sarah-Jane Oakenfull

This isn't nice to hear, nor to type, but a lot of obese people feel that way. So when and if they go on to lose weight, it can open doors to new attractions and the marketplace becomes bigger and more varied. After being in a smaller range, sexual attractively speaking, suddenly you are more visible for becoming smaller, you are contradicting from the other side, no longer the biggest in society and invisible. Smaller but more noticed. It can be an amazing feeling to be noticed and appreciated by others in that way after being so transparent.

Sadly, statistically the divorce rate after weight-loss surgery is high, as is separation. No one, whatever size should have to feel like they need to just settle. Everyone deserves the right to be loved and to love in return.

I guess I am one of the lucky ones that seem to have escaped that sad statistic, thus far. My husband with his sexy, sarcastic, spectrum way of looking at life is still completely unbothered by my appearance and not one bit jealous nor afraid that I'll do a moonlight flit with some younger hunk. He often tells me I look nice. We look back at pictures and we both say that we can't believe it was the same me. He shows me he is proud of me and voices that at times. He often looks at me and asks, "What the fuck are you wearing now?" if I bounce down the stairs in a yellow jumper and dungarees, with little frilly socks on and a ribbon in my hair, "You look like a minion, Sarah." He found my new haircut with fringe a great source of humour, particularly when I got myself some new super funky small, perfectly circular glasses. "You look like Edna from *The Incredibles*," followed by a dry bout of laughter. My response... "Heeellllo Daarrrlinggg".

Bypassing Obesity

The thing about living with someone who is incredibly dry and literal is that you always seem to get the truth. I don't really give a shit if he hates my outfits as long as I love them. Has my weight loss impacted our relationship? Yes, how can it not? It some ways it has been strengthened. Sex is certainly much easier, and success can be achieved in a more aerobic manner. We argue mainly about the children, he being very strict and steady, and me being a free spirit. I do much more round the house by way of DIY now days. I get involved and am no longer the hammer passer or tool provider. When I have cut the grass, it no longer wipes me out for the day, I just get on with next job. So I think me being more able-bodied has made his life a bit easier, although because of his structure and need for routine in life, it may well put him out of sync with me just flitting around from job to job like a child that has had its first taste of freedom.

We seem, at the moment at least, to be happy and healthy in our relationship, one based on respect and love above anything else.

Moving on to friendships, primarily my most prevalent one and that is with Helen. I am now slim, and Helen is still in shape, round is a shape, right? I know she won't be offended by that, because she told me write it. Helen is still obese. Has it changed our friendship? I think we both thought it might do, as we were binge buddies. Sometimes it felt like food was the glue binding us together.

She was fully supportive, as always, of me having bariatric surgery. Being fat together was like being in a club I guess, both of us being active and shunning the usual stereotypes associated with obesity. We dressed differently, but always out of the ordinary realms of the typical fat woman. Helen dresses like a teenager, she dons T shirts with cartoon characters on and wears crocs (the holes in those things are where your dignity seeps out), I always wore dresses or trousers with layers of tops, scarves and accessories.

Sarah-Jane Oakenfull

Mine and Helen's relationship is like no other, we are like a married couple. We think the same and don't have sex, the only thing that is missing with our marriage is arguments as we have never in thirty years had one. Helen has no children and thinks of my daughters as her own, and they in turn call her second mum. Most people assume we are a partnership and they are not wrong in many ways. She is my go-to in all situations, my love for her is concrete.

We are the same today as we were three years ago. We speak most days, even if it's just to hear each other breathe as we often don't have anything much exciting to say. I thought that the dynamics of our relationship might change as I did but I'm so glad to say they did not.

Once, when Helen walked in and saw me in a dress, she burst into tears of joy and she treats me no differently now than she did before. That is true love.

My family are an eclectic bunch. We have branches from our family tree that have branches growing from them and so on. My little sister (taller than me and seventeen years my junior) brought me a new dress in a size twenty from Primark. That day was so special as I had never been bought clothes before from my family.

My sister is really slim, and I have always been envious of her, now I can almost steal her clothes. All my brothers are very proud of me, and we are pretty close. Nothing has changed with our relationships at all, they are still arseholes, and I am still always late to every family occasion.

Bypassing Obesity

Mumma Sange, my best mate and my life giver. Our relationship has changed but that's not necessarily a bad thing. As I started to lose weight and could fit in her clothes, a few garments didn't see their way back to her wardrobe. Then I became smaller than her and at times she has struggled with that. Although she is very proud and incredibly supportive, she has made many a comment about feeling envious. The most important thing is that she is relieved that my health and physical abilities have improved. This is mainly due to mum's health worsening and me being able to help her more around the house, taking her shopping without moaning that my feet are too swollen to keep walking. We are a close team, mum and I, the shift in dependency is happening now as she gets older, and I'm pleased that I'm able-bodied enough to provide that care.

My mum loves to tell people that I used to be obese and will tell any and everyone about it. The cashier in the supermarket, the postman or just a random stranger in a queue. She is very proud indeed. I often raise my eyes to the skies when she starts telling all and sundry about her daughter's weight-loss. The changes within our relationship are minimal but on the whole they are all positive ones, minus the stolen clothes.

Lozza and Cazza, dad and step mum. The pair that provided me with the tool. This relationship has changed also. A deep gratitude and respect have bloomed. My Dad looks at me differently now. I can't explain how, but there has been a change. I think maybe he has a deepened respect for me, as I have for him. I know he is extremely proud of me and again, as a parent, he is feeling a relief that I am now free of the burden that obesity caused me. I guess that when you have given someone that much money, it must be satisfying to see the physical change it has made.

For years I was committed to disliking my step mum, I think maybe out of loyalty to my mum. Time goes by and sometimes instead of carrying the ugliness of resent, we have to see the bigger picture and except that we were wrong.

Sorry Cazza.

Sarah-Jane Oakenfull

The bond between parent and child is as strong as it gets. Losing obesity doesn't change that at all. It has, however strengthened the respect and allowed some of the worries my parents had for me to diminish. It's a really profound feeling to know you have not only unburdened yourself but also your beloved parents too.

TWENTY-TWO

Hard work and charity

I could most probably write a whole book on the positives of surviving and combating obesity but alas it would be a bit boring and kick in the teeth to all those are desperately trying to battle with the disease. Knowing how difficult it is to overcome it, I completely understand.

The NHS are so very overwhelmed, particularly after Covid. However, there are many different routes that could be tapped into for the battle against obesity and ultimately human beings are being let down by the system. The price for weight-loss surgery is unattainable for most average, working class families and so many people are left feeling trapped not only in their bodies, but in their minds too.

There has to be an answer and I have no idea what that involves, but human beings are suffering whilst carrying obesity, and help is sparse. The mantra of helping yourself is completely and utterly wasted to those with addictions or poor mental health and life as an obese individual is a cycle of despair for the many.

Sarah-Jane Oakenfull

Again, I am humble and will forever be grateful for my chance. The changes physically are some days a secondary thought. As day-to-day life creeps in and you start to live the new life, you can almost forget that you are no longer obese. Yes, it is far easier to move and thrive but eventually that freedom becomes normalised.
On occasion, I have walked past a shop window, caught a glimpse of myself and for a split second not recognised myself and been really shocked momentarily. In some photos, where maybe I'm in the background, it takes time for the brain to catch up and realise that the slim person I see is really me.

Lots of people who have had dramatic weight loss have reported having a type of body dysmorphia. The weight is coming off and the clothes are shrinking but yet all they see in the mirror is an overweight or obese person staring back at them. Despite any amounts of kind words and compliments it can be really hard to see just how far you have come. I always took lots of pictures when I was obese, I was never camera shy so I have plenty of photos that enable me to compare if ever I feel like I need to.

I do sometimes feel like I have imposter syndrome. I feel like I don't belong in the aisles of smaller clothes, or in the high street stores. In my adult life there have only ever been a few shops that sold my size, so I have not been privy to the trendier shops in town. I think that's another reason for my love of charity shops, the possibility of browsing and never having an idea of what I'm going to find.

Through all the changes in this journey of morbid obesity diminishing, the one that I struggle with most is the way in which people, everyday people in the street, strangers, now treat me. People are kinder to me now and that makes me both angry and sad. I have the door held open for me by strangers now. People will hold the lift door for me in department stores.

Just lately I have completely run with my new life, and I have had opportunities and possibilities that have come my way. I feel very deeply in my heart that I have been blessed.

Bypassing Obesity

After the first year of life after WLS and heading towards the eighteen-month marker, I bit the bullet. I go into my local charity warehouse a few times a week. It is my sanctuary and my hobby. With my changes in size, I have been able to kit out my wardrobe completely and utterly from sustainable, preloved, and best of all very inexpensively.

I started to have a rapport with the staff, and they suggested that I join them and become a volunteer. I hadn't worked since the girls were very young and certainly not in a shop, let alone a huge warehouse full of treasure. I was so nervous. I applied and was accepted to join the hospice as a volunteer.

It was the best, okay second, no third, (having my children, overcoming obesity) best thing I have ever done for me.

The people I worked with are amazing. The charity is beyond incredible, and I really felt like I was doing good in the world. Not just for the charity but for the community too. The warehouse is really, really affordable, the tops are just £1 for example. The furniture sells for such a reasonable price that even the smallest of budgets are able to attain. Everything we sell is affordable and affordable to the masses.

I had been there a few months doing the odd afternoon or morning when a job position came up. The warehouse was being separated into two units and so one would become a homeware unit and the other would be for fashion. They were looking for an assistant manager to join the team.

I applied.

I've never done anything like that before, but I had some knowledge from my volunteering. Above all I have a respect for the charity alongside a huge passion for the sustainable fashion and reusing items. I love that place. I only bloody got the job.

Sarah-Jane Oakenfull

My interview went well and so I was offered the job the very same day. I was an assistant manager at my beloved charity shop, I was so proud of myself. As a customer I used to have little ideas about how to display the clothes and keep everything looking as good as it can be, and now I'm doing it and doing it as a career.

Every day I am helping make the charity money and helping the local community. I am part of an incredible team of people from all walks of life that come together with the sole purpose of making money for the charity. The only downside is that I have more clothes and shoes than Elton blooming John.

If I have any advice to anyone stuck in a rut, find somewhere to volunteer and become part of a team. It really can help with mental health as well as helping the charity.

My job has helped me far more than I could ever help them. It has helped me establish who I am, now that I am no longer Fat Sarah. Before, people just saw an obese woman, most probably thought I was a lazy cow that stuffed her face all day happily. That was never me, the true me was a woman that had a deep unhappiness within her but was trapped by her weight and trapped in her own mind. Now I am free, no longer incarcerated by my own body, a body of my own making, all be it subconsciously so.

This freedom is a privilege and a deliverance, and I am so grateful for it. At work I am simply Sarah. I hope I am still kind and hard-working. I am true to myself and my core beliefs, but I am no longer seen as a fat person, just a regular a person without the label of obesity.

My job has given me hope for the future away from motherhood, away from autism, away from the housework. My weight-loss has given me a life without restrictions. A life that is limitless and independent.

TWENTY-THREE

The skin I live in

The pure heat of a flame melts the wax in the candle. It turns the solid in to liquid, one that oozes southwards, down towards the earth. After beginning its purpose as a solid form, the wax, under heat, can no longer contain its mass and therefore gives in to the warmth and becomes a fluid, flowing and transforming into something new. This transformation is not lost on me. The end result of losing fourteen stone in weight and dropping ten dress sizes, is very similar to that of the melted, molten candle wax.

A spark inside me was lit. It became a flame and the wax melted, transformed and became dripping layers of dissolved and disused skin. Skin which was once solid and had been for a considerable length of time. The heat from the spark started a chain reaction both mentally and physically.

Mentally, I am the flame, I am the heat and the driving force behind the reaction. I feel, most days, as fierce and powerful as that flame, pushing forwards to melt the wax and turn the solid into the liquid. I am altering molecules and doing science.

Sarah-Jane Oakenfull

Physically, I am the wax. I was the solid mass for a long time. Hard and formed, I thought at some points in my life like I would forever be that way. Once the spark was conceived and full flame overtook it was inevitable that the liquefied wax would settle and become what is now lose skin. A forever reminder of the burden (obesity) I carried. Lose skin is, and I cannot lie nor ignore it, bittersweet. It is a bit like having a new car with rusty body work. The engine is good and reliable, it starts first time, every time. With a service and some tender loving care the car is going to get you to your destination and last you, until you no longer need it. The body work needs work aesthetically, but it doesn't affect the ride.

To be frank, I look like I have melted. The skin is hanging from me like a leech. It hangs down from every available part of my body. My arms have wings, not like an old lady but much, much worse. The skin from my arms hangs down about three inches, it is soft and warm, like dough. It has wrinkles and stretch marks, it is not smooth but almost lined like a barcode, a receipt for my morbid obesity. My tummy is still sizeable, the empty sack that once housed the burden is still there, a reminder, a warning. My boobs that once were the size of my head are now dangly and empty. They have been abandoned and rejected like a sad puppy. I could almost roll them up like a dormant sleeping bag. My legs are what I dislike the most. My thighs were very, very big, the worst area by far. Now they are sacks of wrinkles and drips of stretched and empty skin, like fluid wax. If you imagine the amount of excess weight my body was carrying every day and try to visualise the skin being pulled taught, extended, almost to capacity. Like a balloon being inflated beyond its intended volume, leave the balloon to deflate, then notice the scar and deformation it leaves in place of the air. That is what my thighs have become after losing 199lbs of fat.

Bypassing Obesity

I have spoken to many people have lost weight and been left with the bittersweet by-product of excess skin. Some feel as if it is a badge of honour, a reminder that they have overcome and beaten obesity. Others feel like it is a punishment, a sentence for their crimes to their bodies. Some have had the invasive, serious surgery to have the skin removed. This is both expensive and has a long recovery time, not dissimilar to a Caesarean section. I can see both points of view and some days I felt extremely lucky and brave, I would show my skin. Maybe not the saggy breasts or the swing that my vagina now has, but the arms and some thigh and I feel empowered and proud.

Other days I feel sad that, after the journey I have been on and the struggles that I have overcome, I am still living with the constant reminder of morbid obesity. I feel upset and angry at myself as I stand and evaluate the aftermath. I see my body though a stranger's eyes and could weep. I would have the skin removed and my boobs up and perky in a heartbeat on those dull days. Overall my main train of thought is how incredibly lucky I have been, how lucky I am. Gratitude for my new life far overtakes any diluted joy and when I am having a bad moment, I am forever humble. If an opportunity ever comes my way, and that equates to funds and family situations, I think I would have some construction surgery done but as of yet the chance has not arisen.

Living in the skin I am in far outweighs the skin I had when obese. Being able to physically 'do' with ease is to me the best of all the doors that bypassing obesity has opened. The skin is and always will be a reminder of my burden. A visual cue to myself that I was one of the lucky ones. I will never not be obese, in my heart and soul. I am a survivor, an advocate, and an ally forever. When you have lived a life feeling trapped in a body of your own making, subconsciously; when you have been put into a box by a society and shunned, shamed and judged, how can you ever forget that?

I will never let anyone berate obesity. I am a voice and my words are my weapon against the treatment of those who are suffering in silence with an addiction, or poor mental health, and those who are suffering, and they are, of obesity.

To those that know and love a human being carrying the burden of obesity: just as you cannot heal a wound or cure an addiction, you cannot shame or 'tough love' someone into losing weight. In fact it could make it a heavier burden and harder one to overcome. All the help an obese person needs from you is love and understanding.

There is no easy answer and there is no easy fix. Like any addict, it has to come from a place of complete determination and self-love, of self-worth. Those are not emotions that come easily when you carry morbid obesity.

To support someone is to first listen. To recognise that this, this heaviness, this load, is not ever a conscious decision. No one would ever choose to live a life with restrictions and boundaries.

Morbid obesity is not an aspiration or ambition. It is a subconscious action and is often out of the carrier's control.

I said at the beginning of my story that this is not one of weight-loss surgery endorsement nor one of pontification about losing weight. It is simply my story, my life and my badly spelt words.

I have bypassed obesity, but I want people to know what it is to live in a body carrying obesity. I want obese people to know that in any situation there is always hope, there is always someone to listen and to understand you. I found my way out, there is a way out if you want it, but you have to love yourself first. You are important. You are worth saving.

Well that is almost me up to date.

I am Sarah. I am a morbidly obese woman in recovery and right now the recovery is more than I could ever have imagined. I was worth it, and you are too.

They say it ain't over until the fat lady sings. She sang years ago, at every opportunity. The fat lady was me, and she's physically gone now so that's it.

Bypassing Obesity

The end.

Fuck it, Who am I kidding?

This is just the beginning.

Sarah-Jane Oakenfull

Printed in Great Britain
by Amazon